L.I.F.E.
Leadership Solutions

Before You Ever Had The Problem,
God Had The Solution.

RSI
PUBLISHING

by Billy Durham

Scriptures are taken by permission from the ESV (English Standard Version) KJV (King James Version of the Bible), NKJV (New King James Version), NLT (New Living Translation), AMPC (Amplified Bible Classic Edition), AMP (Amplified Bible Translation), and CEV (Contemporary English Version)

RSIP
Raising the Standard International Publishing L. L. C.
https://www.rsipublishing.com
The front cover image was designed by
Asher Durham

Books may be ordered through booksellers or by contacting Billy Durham:
billydurham3@gmail.com
www.johncmaxwellgroup.com/billydurham

Disclaimer Statement:

This book contains general Biblical and personal information based on the author's knowledge and experiences from God's Word and his Christian walk. It is published for general reference purposes only to bless others.

The publisher and the author disclaim any personal liability, either directly or indirectly, for the information contained within this Bible study. Although the publisher and the author have made every effort to ensure the accuracy and completeness of the information contained within this Bible study, we assume no responsibility for errors, inaccuracies, omissions, and inconsistencies.

ISBN: 9781960641670

Printed in the United States of America
Edition Date: January 2025

Table of Contents

Week Six – Essentials for Living in Faithful Excellence

-Afterword-
The Ultimate L.I.F.E. Leadership Solution

-Appendix-
Tools and Additional Resources

Acknowledgments

I would like to thank my wife, Sherri, for her love, patience, encouragement, and wisdom as I sought her insight and feedback on much of the content of this book over the years that I have been putting it together. She is my most precious gift from God, my best friend, and the greatest blessing in my life.

I would also like to thank Dr. Bill Jones for writing the forward and being an incredible model and a mentor to me, someone who leads his life with faithful excellence in so many areas. God has blessed me to have an abundance of other men and women in my life, too many to name here, who have also modeled the highest levels of leadership for me, investing and imparting in me in numerous ways. I cannot thank them all enough!

Lastly, I would like to thank my son Asher Durham for the cover design, Charles Morris for all his encouragement and "gentle prodding," and other close friends who continued to hold me accountable to go the distance on this labor of love. You know who you are, and without you, this book would not have been possible. So, with gratitude and joy, I acknowledge you all!

Foreword

I have had the privilege of knowing Billy Durham for four decades now. We met at a large youth conference the week after Christmas in 1982. Billy, serving as a youth minister at that point, brought a large group of students. I was one of the conference speakers. For some reason, God was pleased to connect us, and one of those rare life-long friendships was born.

In 1986, Billy gave me the honor of officiating his wedding to Sherri. That happens to be a miracle, not just that she is so much godlier than he is, but from the perspective that I had pushed hard for him to marry someone else! For Sherri to want me to officiate their ceremony had to be miraculous, or at least close to it. In my defense, I did not know Sherri at the time. I know of no stronger woman of prayer than she.

Having the same passion for making Christ famous among the nations, Billy and I tried several times to work together. It happened once, though briefly. Only a few months after Billy arrived, I left to start Crossover Global, an organization that plants churches among Muslims and Hindus. In spite of being separated by distance geographically for the majority of our forty-year friendship, we have remained close relationally.

I share this history to let you know that I know Billy; I know him well. As a result, I can say that he's the real deal. He lives a "life in faithful excellence." Everyone who knows him will vouch for his Christ-centered life. They will bear witness to his godly family. They will underscore his effective ministry.

This is important to me because I don't want to read a devotional written by someone who only knows the Word of God. I only have so much time, so I want to read a devotional written by someone who not only knows the Word of God but also intimately knows the God of the Word. He has learned from years of personal experience that long before he ever had a problem, the God of Scripture had the solution.

This brings us to this beneficial book written by Billy. L.I.F.E. Leadership Solutions provides six weeks of potentially life-changing exhortations filled with stories, quips, biblical insights, and practical applications. You will not only gain a deeper perspective on a biblical worldview, but you will have fun doing it.

One warning, however. Resist the temptation to cover more than one chapter per day. Take the time to marinate in each day's lesson. Make this journey a spiritual exercise, not simply an intellectual one. Allow the Holy Spirit the time it takes to affect life change. You will be glad you did.

Dr. Bill Jones
President of Columbia International University
Co-founder and President of Crossover Communications International

Introduction

Have You Ever Had A Problem?

If you have lived on this planet for any amount of time, let's assume that the answer is "yes"? Have you ever had a month, a week, a day, or even a few hours without needing a solution to at least one problem? Congratulations! You are officially qualified to read this book and probably even write a few chapters. Just dealing with the day-to-day demands in our own lives provides plenty of challenges, obstacles, setbacks, and opportunities to overcome. This book will guide you through the treacherous waters of problem-solving, turning you from a hapless bystander into a fearless, solution-oriented leader.

Where Do You Go To Find Solutions?

Life can be messy at times. It's full of unexpected challenges, from leaky faucets to global pandemics. These are leading your personal life, your marriage, your family, your work life, your social life, and more. But fear not, dear reader! Within you lies the potential to rise to the occasion, to transform from ordinary Joe (or Jane) into an extraordinary problem-solver. This book is written to equip you with the tools and insight to conquer some of life's obstacles, no matter how daunting. So, roll up your sleeves, put on your cape (or at least a decent pair of pants), and let's get to work finding solutions.

Before You Ever Had The Problem, God Had The Solution.

What Is The Best Way To Read This Book And Get The Most Out Of It?

This book is a humble attempt to share some of what I've gleaned from the wisdom of God in the Bible and through the years of my walk with Him, sometimes stumbling along the way but continually seeing His faithfulness to provide solutions. If there is one thing I do know after 66 times around the sun, it's this – Before I ever had the problem, God had the solution! The format is written as a daily devotional with a problem, a solution, and the Truth, which is a scripture reading to prompt reflective prayer over what you have read for that day. On the seventh day of each week, it breaks away from the problem, solution, and scripture reading format to provide space to write out and journal (reflect, record, and rejoice) any specific takeaways from that week. To get the most from this book, I encourage you to give space for that to happen, even if it is 5, 10, or 15 minutes. So, whether you're a seasoned problem-solving leader or a total novice, join me on this adventurous journey to discover some L.I.F.E. (Living In Faithful Excellence) Leadership Solutions.

Week One - Day One
Solutions For L.I.F.E.
Who Needs Solutions?

The Problem

Maybe you heard the joke about the executive who sent out the following memo; *"It has come to my attention that every time we solve one problem, we create two more. From now on, all problem-solving is prohibited!"* The fact that life is full of problems is the very reason we need a book about solutions. Health problems, work problems, school problems, marriage problems, family problems, relational problems, pet problems, traffic problems, and the list goes on and on. Here a problem, there a problem, everywhere a problem, problem; (sing it with me) "Old Macdonald had a problem, e-i-e-i-o." Problems are essentially a part of life, so in a sense, we wouldn't experience a full life without some problems. If you have experienced that life will inevitably have some amount of adversity and challenges, then finding solutions becomes even more critical. It's been proven through behavioral science studies that there is a physiological release of satisfaction and happiness when we find solutions to our problems. Finding solutions is an essential skill that helps us navigate life's challenges and overcome obstacles. The problem only seems to grow when our struggle to find a solution creates an even greater problem. That's when you meet that person who says, *"Of course, I'm doing something about the problem – I'm avoiding it!."* That is not a solution! As the saying goes, never ask a drowning person to show you how to swim.

Before You Ever Had The Problem, God Had The Solution.

If we can agree that life has problems and solutions are good, then it would stand to reason that we all need solutions from time to time. I know I do, and I would imagine you do too. Here's my question; "Are you part of the problem, part of the solution, part of the problem with the solution, or part of the solution to the problem with the solution?" Now, that is a problem that needs a solution!

The Solution

In Psalm 27:5, David talks about a problem he had and the solution he found. He called it "the day of trouble." I have had a few "days of trouble" in my life, and I imagine you have too. His solution was "to find shelter in the secret place of God's presence." Because of his relationship with God, he had confidence that God would be his refuge in his day of trouble. Where do you go in your day of trouble? When do you need life solutions? Is your solution found in a person? Is it in a philosophy, a theology, a teaching, or a book? This book you are reading now is about giving some solutions to some of the problems that many people face in life at some point. I have found that most solutions are simple, though not always easy. You will read that statement quite a bit in the following pages. You will also discover that I go to a specific source and what I consider the greatest book ever written for solutions in my life. The person is God the Father, by way of His Son, Jesus Christ, and through the power of the Holy Spirit who lives in me.

The greatest book ever written that I have referred to is the Holy Bible, which is the living word of God. This is no ordinary book; I will explain more as you keep reading. It is the greatest source of wisdom, understanding, knowledge, and solutions for every area of life. Because God is the ultimate source of solutions in life, knowing Him makes all the difference. He even offers to give us His wisdom to solve every problem we face if we simply ask Him!

> James 1:5-7 NLT says, "If you need wisdom, ask our generous God, and He will give it to you. He will not rebuke you for asking."

Simply Ask! Wow, that's it? Well, that is what His word says. The other problem is that we want a solution to our problems now, and we want the wisdom we need ASAP. It's one of those things we can't seem to get quick enough. This is where I want to challenge you to give yourself some listening time each day.

> Psalm 46:10 AMPC says, "Let be and be still, and know that I am God...."

I like this "Amplified Classic" translation because it emphasizes that we must give our lives some "still time" and intentionally "let be." If you struggle with this idea, then you are like most people. We have so many demands for our attention, from when we wake up to when our heads hit the pillow. It may feel a little awkward at first but as you practice a little "be still" time, I believe you will see the benefit of it soon. The "Let be" part is to take time to let go of your own striving or stress, pressure or worry, trouble or problem, and just know that He is God *and* has the solution you need. Notice the top of every even-numbered page of this book, **"Before you ever had the problem, God had the solution!"** I truly believe that statement, and my goal in writing this book is to help you believe it, too.

The Truth

Each day, we will take a few minutes (aka "Let be and be still" time) to fill our minds and hearts with some truth from God's word. See, we are already making deposits of wisdom for the solutions you will need. After reading the following verses, jot down your thoughts on what these verses say about solutions for problems, struggles, challenges, and trouble.

Psalm 46:1

John 14:27

John 16:33

Philippians 4:6-7

1 Peter 5:7

Week One – Day Two
Solutions For L.I.F.E.
Are You Winning The Game Of Life?

The Problem

Have you ever played the actual game of Life? Yes, I'm talking about The Game of Life, also known simply as "Life," which is a board game created in 1860 by Milton Bradley. The game simulates a person's travels through their life, from early adulthood to retirement, with the possibility of college, jobs, marriage, and even children along the way. The modern version was originally published 100 years later, in 1960, and was "heartily endorsed" by media and television personality Art Linkletter. It is now part of the permanent collection of the Smithsonian's National Museum of American History and an inductee into the National Toy Hall of Fame. They have continued to add multiple versions over the years, including an arcade and online option. As they say, "Life just goes on."

However, real life is not always as problem-free as a board game; it usually includes real problems, real people, real money (or lack thereof), and other realities. I believe it was Herbert Hoover who said, "As soon as we can make ends meet, somebody moves the ends." The word "L.I.F.E." in this book title is written that way for a reason, and it stands for "Living In Faithful Excellence." That can be a challenge and a problem. Not the living part so much but the "faithful" and "excellence" part. However, some people do struggle with the living part. The good news is that we each get the same number of minutes to live each day, so we can choose how to invest those minutes. Every choice you make makes up your collective life, so the key is to choose carefully to have the life you desire. Therefore, it is vital to determine for yourself what does and what doesn't matter each day. Always remember, you and I are rich with the power of choice. Yes, there may be some limitations or boundaries you live under, but for the most part, we each get to decide. I'm reminded of the lyrics of a song from one of my favorite bands, Switchfoot, "This is your life, is it who you want to be?" (More on that in the Week Two, Day One devotional)

The Solution

Defining moments can change the direction of your life. Life can turn on a dime, so to speak, without you having any control over what is happening. To make the life you desire most happen, I suggest a good place to start is to determine your preferred direction in advance. In other words, today is the future you looked forward to 10 years ago. That can be a somewhat staggering thought. The choices you have made and the direction you chose at each life intersection have all brought you to this place. The millions of decisions to stop or go, coast or persevere, pull back in fear, or press on in faith are the sum of what or who you have become. That can either be good news or not-so-good news. Part of the solution is found in one of my favorite quotes by C.S. Lewis: *"You can't go back and change the beginning, but you can start where you are and change the ending!"* Here is a good question to ask ourselves in finding a solution to this challenge in life: What do I need to do now so that I am not living in regret 5, 10, or 15 years from now? Where do I need to grow personally? Where do I need to invest my time relationally? What matters most?

These questions get us down to the essentials. I recently read this statement, which caused me to ask some big questions about my life. *"If you only had one month (week or day) to live, you would be surprised by all the things that really don't matter anymore."* This doesn't mean we abandon our responsibilities and just do whatever feels right at the moment, but it does lead us to consider our core values and make decisions that reinforce those values. I encourage you to keep this in mind - choose wisely, and your decisions will reward you; choose unwisely, and your decisions will rob you. Let's go after some wisdom today from the word of Truth!

The Truth

Consider the following scriptures from God's word for wisdom to move forward in finding solutions for making decisions that lead you to the life that reflects God's best for you.

1. **The foundation for every wise decision – Proverbs 1:7**

2. **The difference between wisdom and understanding – Proverbs 1:1-5**

3. **The Source of Wisdom – Proverbs 2:6-7**

4. **Making decisions in the gray areas – I Corinthians 10:24-33**

5. **Godly Wisdom vs. Worldly Wisdom – James 1:5; 3:13-18**

Week One – Day Three
Solutions For L.I.F.E.
Does It Have To Be So Complicated?

The Problem

Do you remember the series of AT&T "It's Not Complicated" commercials that featured children sitting around a kid's classroom with an adult asking them questions? The kids would give these hilarious, often somewhat complicated answers, and then the voiceover would say, "It's not complicated...better is better." The hilarious part about this promo is that in some of my dealings with AT&T, it can sometimes get unnecessarily complicated. I always liked the way Charles Schultz, the writer of the comic strip Peanuts, would make simple, uncomplicated, funny statements about life through Linus, Lucy, Charlie Brown, and the other characters of the comic strip "Peanuts." Some of my favorites were:

- **"I love mankind...It's people I can't stand."**
- **"I have a new philosophy. I'm only going to dread one day at a time."**
- **"Sometimes I lie awake at night and ask, 'Where have I gone wrong,' then a voice says to me, 'This is going to take more than one night.'"**

That last one shows how complicated life can get sometimes. However, most leadership solutions for life do not have to be complex, or at least not as difficult as we tend to make them. Everyone finds themselves in leadership opportunities every day. Leadership author and expert John Maxwell says the most complex person to lead is the person looking back at you in the mirror. Self-leadership is thrust upon all of us, whether we think we're a leader or not. You get to lead your thoughts in a particular direction, which leads to the words you say and, ultimately, your actions and reactions in life. Again, it's not complicated. However, it takes a concerted effort to be intentional about leading your life, even more so if you're leading a family, in the workplace, through a church, an organization, or the community. It also takes something very practical and spiritual called *self-discipline*.

The Solution

The Bible talks about *self-discipline* (some versions say *self-control*), referring to it as one of the Fruit of the Spirit in **Galatians 5:22-23**. Also, in 2 **Timothy 1:7,** we are told that God gives us a spirit of *self-discipline* (again, some versions say *self-control* or *sound mind*). So, one solution to many leadership problems is the beautiful and powerful spiritual fruit of *self–discipline*. You might want to simplify it even more by saying self-discipline is vital to self-leadership.

For personal growth, it's been said that a good rule of thumb is simply focusing on improving 1% daily. It also sounds astronomical if you get to the end of one year and have improved by 365% from the previous year. Wait, what? That is like comedian Stephen Wright's math when it comes to aging. He quips, "When I turned two, I was really anxious because I'd doubled my age in a year. I thought, if this keeps up, by the time I'm six, I'll be ninety."

Let's keep this solution simple by saying that with self-leadership, one should never underestimate the importance of *self-discipline*. I'm not saying you pull yourself up by your own bootstraps and just gut it out. The best *self-discipline* for self-leadership is the "Holy Spirit empowered gift from God" kind. All the best solutions come from God, and in His goodness, as we submit to His work in our lives, we find the best solutions for *self-discipline* with our self-leadership. It's saying "yes" to choices that lead you to be the person you want to be and "no" to any decisions that lead you to the person you don't want to be. Again, it's not complicated, but it's also not always easy. We'll talk more about our choices another day, but today, let's look at some truths from God's word about that amazing character quality known as *self-discipline*.

The Truth

> *I Corinthians 9:24-27 NKJV "Do you not know that those who run in a race all run, but one receives the prize? Run in such a way that you may obtain it. And everyone who competes for the prize is temperate in all things. Now they do it to obtain a perishable crown, but we for an imperishable crown. Therefore I run thus: not with uncertainty. Thus I fight: not as one who beats the air. But I discipline my body and bring it into subjection, lest, when I have preached to others, I myself should become disqualified.*

> *2 Timothy 1:7 AMP "For God did not give us a spirit of timidity or cowardice or fear, but [He has given us a spirit] of power and of love and of sound judgment and personal discipline [abilities that result in a calm, well-balanced mind and self-control]."*

Before You Ever Had The Problem, God Had The Solution.

Galatians 5:22-23 AMP "But the fruit of the Spirit [the result of His presence within us] is love [unselfish concern for others], joy, [inner] peace, patience [not the ability to wait, but how we act while waiting], kindness, goodness, faithfulness, gentleness, self-control. Against such things there is no law."

Week One – Day Four
Solutions For L.I.F.E.
What Is Faithfulness?

The Problem

One of the biggest problems you will face regularly is the temptation to get discouraged by being overwhelmed by the battles we face each day. As author and pastor Mark Batterson has said, "You never know what relationship, skill, experience or attribute God will use to bring about His eternal purposes." Consider these examples:

- **For Esther, it was a beauty pageant to stop the genocide of the Jewish nation.**
- **For Nehemiah, it was his relationship with the king as a cupbearer that gave him the favor he needed for his mission.**
- **For David, the shepherd boy, it was his musical skill that got him into the palace.**
- **For Joseph, it was his supernatural gift to interpret dreams.**
- **For Paul, it was his ability to write letters to churches that eventually became a large part of our New Testament Bible.**

If God used them, He can use you. He desires to use you as well. God has placed in you various talents, skills, and abilities to advance His kingdom and fulfill your purpose in life. However, it's up to you to discover, develop, and use what He has given you, and that is when you find the real joy.

It is not always easy and requires your intentional effort to see it come to pass. Faithfulness is what you do with what has been given to you. It's also often referred to as *"stewardship."* It's simply being a steward of what you have been given. Another way I like to say it is, "Do the best you can with what you have where you are."

The Solution

One of the parables of Jesus, known as the parable of the talents, paints this picture with great clarity. It's found in Matthew 25:14-30 and Luke 19:11-27. It's basically how three servants are given different amounts of talents (in Matthew 18, talent is a money term). One servant gets five talents, one gets two talents, and the third servant gets one talent. The two servants with five and two talents are good stewards, investing money and getting more returns for their master. You could say they took what they were given, developed it, and increased its worth. Unfortunately, the third servant, who had one talent, did nothing with his and was not a good steward. The Master was so upset that he called him "wicked and lazy" and even took his one talent away and gave it to the servant, who now had ten talents. (Ouch! – that would be a use it or lose it scenario).

The story was straightforward then and still clear today – "Do the best you can with what you have where you are." Be faithful with what you have been given because it matters. It matters for you, others, and the One who gives you the talents, skills, and abilities. This is one of the most important solutions for success in life. It's not based on your circumstances, wealth, power (or lack of power), or platform. It's about being faithful with what God places in your hands and before you. It doesn't matter if you are the five-talent person, the two-talent person, or the one-talent person. Again, it's simply what you do with what you have, where you are. I've known many five-talent guys and gals who never developed what was given to them, and they were surpassed by the two-talent and even the one-talent people.

It's a great day in your life when you realize that something as simple as faithfulness can radically change the trajectory of your life, and you deliberately do something about it. I believe it's true that we are all only one decision away from a totally different life. One choice can change everything. However, you can't leave the choice to chance. For your life to make the best trajectory to the best future, your choices must be based on God's truth for that future. One of the saddest quotes that portray this principle is by George W. Cecil as he states:

"On the plains of hesitation, bleach the bones of countless millions who, at the dawn of victory, sat down to wait, and waiting- died."

But here is the "X Factor" – You must make the call. You must make the move. You must set the goal and the deadline and go for it. Don't get stuck on the plains of hesitation, worried about the outcome or other factors you can't control. Focus on being a faithful steward. How will you be faithful with what you have been given because you have been given so much?

The Truth

Before You Ever Had The Problem, God Had The Solution.

Read the following scripture passages and take a few minutes to write down what you think might be the big idea being communicated. Then, take a minute and write down your gifts or talents, along with how you may be using them now. Thirdly, honestly ask yourself if you are faithful with what God has given you and jot down your answer.

Matthew 18: 14-28 NKJV "For the kingdom of heaven is like a man traveling to a far country, who called his own servants and delivered his goods to them. 15) And to one he gave five talents, to another two, and to another one, to each according to his own ability; and immediately he went on a journey. 16) Then he who had received the five talents went and traded with them, and made another five talents. 17) And likewise he who had received two gained two more also. 18) But he who had received one went and dug in the ground, and hid his lord's money. 19) After a long time the lord of those servants came and settled accounts with them.

20) "So he who had received five talents came and brought five other talents, saying, 'Lord, you delivered to me five talents; look, I have gained five more talents besides them.' 21) His lord said to him, 'Well done, good and faithful servant; you were faithful over a few things, I will make you ruler over many things. Enter into the joy of your lord.' 22) He also who had received two talents came and said, 'Lord, you delivered to me two talents; look, I have gained two more talents besides them.' 23) His lord said to him, 'Well done, good and faithful servant; you have been faithful over a few things, I will make you ruler over many things. Enter into the joy of your lord.'

24) "Then he who had received the one talent came and said, 'Lord, I knew you to be a hard man, reaping where you have not sown, and gathering where you have not scattered seed. 25) And I was afraid, and went and hid your talent in the ground. Look, there you have what is yours.'

26) "But his lord answered and said to him, 'You wicked and lazy servant, you knew that I reap where I have not sown, and gather where I have not scattered seed. 27) So you ought to have deposited my money with the bankers, and at my coming I would have received back my own with interest. 28) Therefore take the talent from him, and give it to him who has ten talents."

1 Peter 4:10 AMP "Just as each one of you has received a special gift [a spiritual talent, an ability graciously given by God], employ it in serving one another as [is appropriate for] good stewards of God's multi-faceted grace [faithfully using the diverse, varied gifts and abilities granted to Christians by God's unmerited favor]."

1. **What are some of my abilities, spiritual gifts, or talents, and how am I using them?**

2. **Am I being faithful to what God has given me? In what specific ways?**

Before You Ever Had The Problem,
God Had The Solution.

NOTES

Week One – Day Five
Solutions For L.I.F.E.
What Is Excellence?

The Problem

Three boys were in the schoolyard, bragging about their fathers. The first boy says, "My dad scribbles a few words on a piece of paper; he calls it a poem, and they give him $150." The second boy says, "That's nothing. My dad scribbles a few words on a piece of paper; he calls it a song, and they give him $500." The third boy says, "I got you both beat. My dad scribbles a few words on a piece of paper; he calls it a sermon, and it takes eight people to collect all the money." Folks, we have a winner!

What comes to your mind when you hear the word excellence? Going the extra mile? Brilliance? Superiority? For some reason, you know excellence when you see it. You also know it when you don't see it. When a company or organization does something with excellence, they stand out from the rest. I think of companies like Chik-fil-A or Disney. You may not like chicken or the "mouse house," but you must admit they did something along the way that produced a significant following. When Walt Disney created his brand of excellence, he called it "plussing" something. It was his own single-minded obsession with excellence. He coined the term "plussing" sometime in the 1940s, long before there was a Disney empire as we know it. He used "plus" as a verb, making it an action word. To "plus" something is to give your customers more than they paid for, more than they expected, and more than you are required to provide them. In this sense, "good enough" was never good enough for Walt Disney, and that became a core value of his commitment to excellence. For example, he plussed Mickey Mouse cartoons with sound when there was no sound in cartoons and continued to be innovative, creative, and relentless in this pursuit of "plussing."

One of the downsides of doing things with excellence is that it usually costs more. Whether it's resources, finances, or manpower, it requires a greater commitment and a different mindset. When you read almost any biography of the Disney brothers, you will see countless examples of a foundational commitment to excellence. Walt was known to say, "You worry about the quality (excellence), let me worry about the cost." (Actually, his brother Roy was the one who worried about the cost). Well, now all of us who go to Disney parks, resorts, cruises, etc., get to worry about the price. Walt would be shocked!

The Solution

So, what about your personal commitment to excellence? What price are you willing to pay to do whatever you do with the highest quality? Rober Madu, pastor, speaker, and digital creator, says, "Jealousy is the trophy that mediocrity gives to excellence." Now that will preach! We seem to be surrounded by mediocrity more than excellence in our world today. Again, good enough is often not good enough. Or, as another AT&T commercial would say, "Just Okay is not Okay"! Is there an area of your life that could use some "plussing"? Often, the small things no one sees lead to the excellence everyone wants. Here lies another simple solution: What you do with excellence today can lead to a more excellent day tomorrow. Along with this, having the right motivation for excellence is essential. Are you pursuing excellence just to impress someone? Or just to get a bigger piece of the pie? That type of reward only lasts briefly. A more excellent motivation will give you the impetus to continue to exceed expectations. **Colossians 3:17** gives us a good motivation for doing things with excellence as it says:

> *Colossians 3:17 "Whatever you do, no matter what it is, in word or deed, do everything in the name of the Lord Jesus, and in dependence on Him, giving thanks to God the Father through Him."*

It's not about trying to impress someone or please a boss or customer, but rather excellence for the Lord and His reward. (see also **Colossians 3:23-24**) Do you see the payoff here? When you do things with excellence or give more than expected in your work, you may not only receive promotions, raises, bonuses, benefits, or some other recognition, but more importantly, you will receive a reward from the One who matters most. When you love more, give selflessly, prefer others, and share generously in your relationships, that excellence will pave the way for you to bless others and be blessed even more!

The Truth

Consider the following scripture passages and ask God to show you specific ways to live and love in "a more excellent way."

Before You Ever Had The Problem,
God Had The Solution.

Colossians 3:23-24 AMP "Whatever you do [whatever your task may be], work from the soul [that is, put in your very best effort], as [something done] for the Lord and not for men, 24 knowing [with all certainty] that it is from the Lord [not from men] that you will receive the inheritance which is your [greatest] reward. It is the Lord Christ whom you [actually] serve."

1 Corinthians 12:31 AMP "But earnestly desire and strive for the greater gifts [if acquiring them is going to be your goal]. And yet I will show you a still more excellent way [one of the choicest graces and the highest of them all: unselfish love]."

Week One – Day Six
Solutions For L.I.F.E.
Is There Only One Solution?

The Problem

There was a struggling manufacturing company in the Midwest that was sensing it was time for a shakeup, so they hired a new CEO. The new boss was determined to rid the company of all slackers and move it forward to greater productivity. On a tour of the facilities, the CEO noticed a guy leaning against a wall. The room was full of workers, and he wanted to let them know that he meant business, so he asked the guy, "How much money do you make a week?" A little surprised, the young man looked at him and said, "I make about $400.00 a week. Why?"

The CEO said, "Wait right here." He walked back into his office, returned in two minutes, handed the guy $1,600.00 in cash, and said, "Here's four weeks' pay. Now GET OUT and don't come back." Feeling pretty good about himself, the CEO looked around the room and asked, "Does anyone want to tell me what that goofball did here?" After a brief pause, a timid voice said, "That was the pizza delivery guy from Papa John's."

I don't think that was the solution the CEO sought to inspire change in the company. The first step is to get clear on the change you want. Author and Career Coach Dan Miller says, "Step one is to create a clear plan, and then steps two through ten (or more) is to take massive action and intentional, consistent steps to work that plan to fruition." A lot of people have hopes and dreams, an "I wish… list" or an "I could've, would've, should've story." Even a "someday, somewhere, If only…" narrative leads to a vague idea of a better future. In this mode, they tend to complain about where they are, point fingers, and blame others for not getting where they think they should be or want to go. This does not have to be your story.

The Solution

Regardless of where you are now, I believe God is more than able to provide the solutions to get you to where you need to be and ultimately want to be. I said solutions plural because there is often more than one possible solution, even though I believe there is one ultimate source. It starts with trusting Him to direct your paths as stated in the ultimate Book of Wisdom, the Bible, in **Proverbs 3:5-6**; "Lean on, trust in, and be confident in the Lord with all your heart and mind and do not rely on your insight or understanding. In all your ways know, recognize, and acknowledge Him, and He will direct and make straight and plain your paths."

There is also a similar passage in **Psalms 37:3-7** that gives even more detail, which we will look at more in "The Truth" for today. It starts with simply trusting God as the source of the solutions and the direction you need. It's being confident in Him for the strength you need and everything else you will need in life, according to **Philippians 4:13** and **19**. When we consider God's promises to supply us with His solutions, we can be encouraged that He will fulfill His word and that His plans, including His solutions for us, are good.

26

Jeremiah 29:11 is an often-quoted verse about God's plans to prosper us, giving us hope and a promising future. The word "prosper" in this verse speaks of our body, soul, and spirit, not just financial prosperity, though it could include that if it is indeed part of His plan for you. However, reading the following verses, 29:12-13, is essential to get the complete picture of the promise.

> *Jeremiah 29:12-13 Then you will call upon Me and go and pray to Me, and I will listen to you. 13) And you will seek Me and find Me, when you search for Me with all your heart."*

So, from this, we see calling on God, praying to Him, and searching for Him with all our heart is the solution to finding and experiencing God's plans for us. When we want the solutions to any problem we are facing, it starts with turning to God and trusting in Him.

The Truth

Take a "be still" moment and think about what these verses say when it comes to trusting God to lead us in His paths, plans, and purposes.

> *Psalms 37:3-5 AMP Trust [rely on and have confidence] in the Lord and do good; Dwell in the land and feed [securely] on His faithfulness. 4 Delight yourself in the Lord, And He will give you the desires and petitions of your heart. 5 Commit your way to the Lord; Trust in Him also and He will do it."*

> *Proverbs 3:5-6 NLT Trust in the Lord with all your heart; do not depend on your own understanding. 6 Seek his*

Before You Ever Had The Problem,
God Had The Solution.

will in all you do, and he will show you which path to take."

Week One – Day Seven
Solutions For L.I.F.E.
Reflect, Record, Rejoice

Reflect

Look back over the past 6 days of devotionals and reflect on what stood out to you from what you read. Did you get any new insight? Any new understanding of God's Word? Did you discover any areas of your life that you need some solutions?

Record

Write down your thoughts from what you just reflected on, putting down any impressions you received on paper. Ask God to give you insight into what He wants to show you from what He has spoken to you this past week.

Rejoice

Express words of thanksgiving to God for His Word, for His desire to speak to you, to lead you, and to give you solutions for living in faithful excellence. Make an intentional effort to find someone today with whom you can share what you learned from your time with God this week! It will most likely encourage them and, in turn, bless you!

Week Two – Day One
Solutions For Leading Your Life
This Is Your Life. Is It Who You Want To Be?

The Problem

This question for today is a line from a song by the band "Switchfoot." This is your life. Is it who you want to be? It is a fundamental question to ask yourself. When I was in college, I heard a campus ministry leader say, "We forfeit 90% of who we are, trying to be someone we're not." It's very easy to fall into that trap, and that's why we need to ask and answer this question. In my L.I.F.E. Leadership Solutions Coaching Business with the John Maxwell Leadership Team, my focus is helping people grow in their personal leadership. This will, in turn, help them to lead better in their marriage and family relationships as well as career, work, ministry, and other areas of life. One of the goals is to coach them to get from where they are to where they want to be by finding solutions that will facilitate that growth. There are no secret formulas or "one size fits all" solutions. However, I found these little not-so-inspirational quips on personal growth funny:

- **You can be anything you want, yet you keep choosing to be you. I admire your dedication to the role.**
- **People come into our lives for a reason; sometimes, that is to make us enjoy being alone.**

31

Before You Ever Had The Problem, God Had The Solution.

- **You are capable of great things. You probably won't do any of them, but you could.**
- **Things didn't work out for a reason, and the reason is that you make terrible decisions.**
- **Stop worrying about what other people think. I mean, have you met other people? They're awful!**

Those are some very non-motivational messages. However, I wouldn't hesitate to say you are where you are today because of the messages you have received from others and the messages you consistently tell yourself. Some would say that the difference between successful people and those who aren't is that successful people ask better questions and, therefore, get better results. So, what kinds of questions are shaping your life? What kind of messaging are you getting consistently? Let's return to the question we started with today; "This is your life. Is it who you want to be?" Now, let's look at a solution.

The Solution

One way we know that questions are important and that asking the right questions is even more important is that Jesus was a master of asking questions. **Matthew 7:7** says, "Ask, and you will receive," so he also encouraged us to ask. Then, in **James 4:2,** it says, "You have not because you ask not." I don't know about you, but I would rather not make that mistake. There is only one way to ask, and that is to pose the question. The way to receive is to ask the question. I would also add that it's not only the questions you ask but also the questions you fail to ask that shape your destiny. Is this the life you want to live? If not, then what are you waiting for, another life? The good news is that you have the incredible power of choice. If you don't like the direction that your life is headed, you can change it, starting today. Here are some basic steps you can start taking now.

1. See Reality

It's like knowing where you are on the map that says, "You are here." Once you find your starting point, you can go where you want to be.

2. Conquer your Fears

Any time you step out to make a change in your life, there will be fears you will have to conquer.

3. Embrace the Process

It will usually be more challenging than you think and take longer than you hoped it would, but it will be worth it in the end.

4. Think Long-term

Almost anyone can accomplish almost anything if they work at it long enough, hard enough, and smart enough. That can be you!

5. Build a Team

Get some people around you and with you who will help you and encourage you to take your life in the direction you desire.

The Truth

Before You Ever Had The Problem,
God Had The Solution.

Luke 11:9 AMP "So I say to you, ask and keep on asking, and it will be given to you; seek and keep on seeking, and you will find; knock and keep on knocking, and the door will be opened to you. For everyone who keeps on asking [persistently], receives; and he who keeps on seeking [persistently], finds; and to him who keeps on knocking [persistently], the door will be opened.

Week Two – Day Two
Solutions For Leading Your Life
Are You Writing Your History To Read As You Desire?

The Problem

The question for today is all about the power of choice. We all have the opportunity to define ourselves according to whatever we choose. Winston Churchill was noted to say, "History will be kind to me, for I will write it so." That's one way to have the story go your way. When AT&T fired CEO John Walter after only 9 months, saying "he lacked intellectual leadership," they gave him a $26 million severance package. His history with AT&T may have initially looked bad, but in the end, it will look favorable on him to get a payout of that amount. Every day, we make choices that write our history. It is the story that we will be known for one day. Simply put, today matters because you are writing more of your story. At the same time, we must be future-minded.

As Stephen Covey introduced in his bestseller, "The Seven Habits of Highly Effective People," we need to have the end in mind to have a better present. It is wise to choose to get on with the future because that is where you are going to spend the rest of your life. If you don't, it's like trying to drive a car looking in the rear-view mirror. At some point, you're going to crash! This is a problem for too many people because they have not learned to think that way. Let's look at a solution.

The Solution

There was a man in the book of Judges named Gideon who sort of re-wrote his history when it was headed in a direction he didn't like. His story opens in Judges 6:11 with him hiding from these people called the Midianites, who were oppressing him and his people to the point that he resorted to beating wheat in a wine press. Yes, you read that correctly, and it's not a great story so far. It was a very low moment in Gideon's life. However, the story is about to take a radical turn as God calls on Gideon to do something epic, heroic, and life-changing.

Don't ever say God doesn't have a sense of humor because he really shows it off in this passage when He sends an Angel with the following greeting to Gideon – "The Lord is with you mighty man of fearless courage" (Judges 6:12). Wait! What? Gideon doesn't look anything like, mighty, fearless, or courageous. This is the first big key in making choices to write your best story. Start to see yourself as God sees you. Gideon saw himself as weak, insignificant, and defeated, but God's view of him was radically different (Judges 6:11-16). Now Gideon had a choice to make - would he continue to write his story as he saw it or as God saw it?

This was a defining moment for Gideon, and as it turns out, it also changed the course of history for the Israelites. We all face similar defining moments in our lives when we have to choose the story we want to write. It may not have the ramifications that Gideon's decision did, but it is nonetheless significant. As you've read before and will read again, you are always one decision away from a different life. This will be good news for Gideon with the decision he makes. Gideon continued down the path of good choices as he stepped out in faith and followed God's voice to tear down some idols, rally God's people, and lead them to defeat those oppressive Midianites. You can read all about it in Judges 6:11- 8:28. He even gets a shout-out in the Hebrews Chapter 11, "Hall of Faith" (Hebrews 11:32-34). I would say he wrote an excellent history for himself! What about you?

The Truth

What will you do today to make choices that will write the history you desire? If the book of your life was finished now, how would it be read? What can you do today to change the narrative to what you would rather it be? What is one thing you could do to get a better view of who you really are according to the way God sees you? Let's start with some Truth from God's Word.

Hebrews 10:35-36 AMP "Do not, therefore, fling away your fearless confidence, for it has a glorious and great reward. For you have need of patient endurance, to bear up under difficult circumstances without compromising, so that when you have carried out the will of God, you may receive and enjoy to the full what is promised."

Psalm 139:13-14 AMP "For You formed my innermost parts; You knit me [together] in my mother's womb. I will give thanks and praise to You, for I am fearfully and wonderfully made; Wonderful are Your works, And my soul knows it very well."

Before You Ever Had The Problem, God Had The Solution.

Hebrews 11:32-34 NLT "How much more do I need to say? It would take too long to recount the stories of the faith of Gideon, Barak, Samson, Jephthah, David, Samuel, and all the prophets. By faith these people overthrew kingdoms, ruled with justice, and received what God had promised them. They shut the mouths of lions, quenched the flames of fire, and escaped death by the edge of the sword. Their weakness was turned to strength. They became strong in battle and put whole armies to flight."

Week Two – Day Three
Solutions For Leading Your Life
Who Is The Toughest Person To Lead?

The Problem

The question for today requires a mirror, for that is where you will find the most challenging person to lead. However, that is where we all have to start if we want to solve this problem, and that is where you will find the most important person to lead. Self-leadership naturally starts with "self," as it begins with taking personal responsibility. No one wants to be like the little boy who wasn't getting good grades in school, and his solution was to approach his teacher with this comment; "I don't want to scare you, but my daddy says if I don't get better grades, somebody is going to get a spanking." Evidently, he didn't get who was responsible for the bad grades, and I would say he was in for a rude awakening.

As John Maxwell says, "You will never change your life until you change something you do daily." Leading yourself is a daily choice you make. Today is the future you looked forward to 10 years, 5 years, even 1 year ago. The choices you have made and the direction you chose at each life intersection have all brought you to this place. The millions of decisions to stop or go, coast or persevere, pull back in fear, or press on in faith are the sum of what or who you have become. Today, you get to lead yourself once again. Which way will you go? Dr. Suess said it best; "You have brains in your head. You have shoes on your feet. You can steer yourself in any direction you choose. Oh, the places you'll go! Except when you don't because sometimes you won't."

The Solution

There was a man in the Old Testament book of Nehemiah by the same name who is an excellent example of how to lead yourself. In Nehemiah 1:4-11, we see several things he did to face a HUGE problem and how self-leadership helped to guide him in the right direction. One of the things he did well was he took the initiative to do some hard things like exercising self-discipline, sacrificing for others, and acting in bold, courageous faith. I've heard it said, "Learn to discipline yourself so someone else doesn't have to." When people demonstrate good self-leadership, they win the respect of others. Regardless of their title (or lack thereof), they will have a platform that enables them to lead others. If Nehemiah had "Seven Secrets of Success," it may have looked something like this:

1. **There is no secret of success**
2. **Success is for everyone**
3. **Your life becomes better only when you become better**
4. **There is no success without sacrifice**
5. **Success is achieved in inches, not miles**
6. **Don't let the greatest enemy of your future success be your past success**
7. **No advice on success works unless you do.**

It's always easier to settle for average than to strive for excellence. Plus, it's easier to be saturated with complacency than stirred with compassion. So, how do you avoid drifting to the lesser way? As author and leadership expert Peter Drucker says, "Feed an opportunity; starve a problem." Opportunities are often born out of problems. Your best opportunities to grow in your self-leadership will frequently be found in the problems you face. Maybe you are facing one right now that will become one of your most significant growth opportunities! Nehemiah had a problem. God provided the solution, and it would require selfless, sacrificial leadership on his part.

The Truth

Helen Keller, who faced more than her share of challenges and obstacles, chose to lead her life in a way that inspired millions. She is often quoted as saying, "Life is either a daring adventure or nothing at all." Where do you need to give more attention to leading that person in the mirror? What can you do today to make a difference in your tomorrow? Read the following scriptures and seek God if there are any areas of your life where you need to take the daring adventure to grow in your leadership.

> *Hebrews 3:15 NLT Remember what it says: "Today when you hear his voice, don't harden your hearts as Israel did when they rebelled."*

> *Nehemiah 4:14 NLT Then as I looked over the situation, I called together the nobles and the rest of the people and said to them, "Don't be afraid of the enemy! Remember the Lord, who is great and glorious, and fight for your brothers, your sons, your daughters, your wives, and your homes!"*

Before You Ever Had The Problem, God Had The Solution.

1 Timothy 4:12 NLT Don't let anyone think less of you because you are young. Be an example to all believers in what you say, in the way you live, in your love, your faith, and your purity.

Week Two – Day Four
Solutions For Leading Your Life
What Is Your Plan To Lead Your Marriage And Family?

The Problem

One of the main areas my wife, Sherri, and I address when doing Marriage (or pre-marriage), Mentoring, and Coaching is communication. I have been known to tell more than one husband this communication advice: "Don't open a can of worms unless you're ready to go fishing." It's often not just what you say, as well as the tone in which you say it, but also what you don't say that matters.

A funny example of this is the story of a couple who were going to marriage counseling, largely because of their inability to communicate and connect after several years of marriage. The wife is pouring out her heart, sharing how her husband never tells her he loves her or shows her affection, while his response to that is, "I told her I loved her on our wedding day, and if something changes, I'll let her know." (I think you see the problem here). So, as the woman continues to pour out her feelings and tears, the counselor gets up, walks across the room, and kisses her on the cheek. Immediately, the woman is shocked but stops crying and feels peace and relief. As the counselor returns to his seat, he looks at the husband and says, "That is what your wife needs every day." After hearing the solution to their problem, the husband looks at the counselor and says, "Well, I can bring her in on

Monday, Wednesday, and Friday, but the other days I'm pretty busy." Clearly, he doesn't get it, and their communication problem isn't even close to being solved, not to mention the counselor's questionable methods!

The second problem we consistently encounter is with expectations. Whether unrealistic, unmet, unfulfilled, or assumed, it can create all sorts of conflict. Things like "I assumed you would pay the bills," "I thought I could just make the final decision on that," "I expected you to be able to fix things like my dad," or "I expected you to be able to prepare meals like my mother." You get the idea. Expectations can cause frustrations, confrontations, and irritations that build up over time, and most expectations come from our experiences in our families of origin. When you're dealing with *uncommunicated* expectations, it gets even more tricky, but the good news is that there are some simple solutions. Let's look at a couple today.

The Solution

For the Solution today, I want to focus on two specific scriptures that I consider to be two "secrets of success" regarding marriage. They are not really secrets since they're in the Bible, but they are often overlooked. The first one is **Ephesians 1:16,** which says, *"I do not cease to give thanks for you, remembering you in my prayers."* The most important thing to communicate to your spouse, apart from your love for each other, is appreciation. When you think grateful thoughts about your spouse, you will tend to say grateful things about them and to them, leading to actions toward your spouse that show gratitude. I know from personal experience in working with hundreds of couples that this is a game-changer. It's simple but not easy, as it requires intentional effort. Combine this effort with the second part of that verse that says, "remembering you in my prayers." Now, I am not talking about praying that God "will fix" your spouse or change them to what you want them to be. However, suppose you are praying consistently and specifically for your spouse that God would bless them and that you would follow God's word for how He says to love each other. In that case, I can guarantee you your relationship will take a radical turn for a more fulfilling marriage. The reason is that you will begin to see them as God sees them, love them with God's heart, and want to serve and prefer them over yourself. One of the best things marriage does for us is to help us die to selfishness. I like to say this to couples. "If you want to expose any selfishness in your life, get married. If that doesn't work, then have kids." You'll begin to see all sorts of stuff in your life that could use the grace of God.

The other verse is **Ephesians 4:15,** which says, *"But speaking the truth in love, both our speech and our lives expressing His truth, let us grow up in all things into Him, following His example who is the head – Christ."* It's so important to speak the truth in our marriage relationships but especially to do that in love! And, when we do this, "We grow up in all things into Him," following the example of Jesus Christ. This is doubly great because we are not only personally maturing in Christ, but our marriage is also growing into its best version. The key to "speaking the truth in love" is humility and preferring one another over yourself. I see so many marriages spiral down when they fail to speak the truth (stop communicating for multiple reasons) or, if they do say it, they don't do it very lovingly. We are all imperfect, and we are married to imperfect human beings. This is where *leading* our thoughts, words, and actions are critical. In marriage, we constantly bump up against our spouses' imperfections. So, how we think about those imperfections, talk about them, and respond to them will determine whether we thrive or just barely survive in marriage.

Here are a few essential keys to remember: believe for the best in each other, allow for honest mistakes, and make forgiveness your default mode. Practice **I Corinthians 13:4-8** in relating each day, then rinse and repeat. Most importantly, remember that you can't love each other the way you need to love each other in your own strength. We are reminded in **Philippians 2:13** when it says, *"For it is not in your own strength, but it is God who is effectively at work in you both to will and do his good pleasure."* It is His pleasure that you have a thriving marriage, and He is willing to work in you and through you to take your marriage there if you will look to Him. As I like to say, you'll never be a *perfect* husband (or wife), but you can be a *praying* husband (or wife). We didn't specifically address parenting and family problems, but I believe the same truth from **Ephesians 1:16, 4:15,** and **Philippians 2:13** applies as well. You will never be a perfect parent, but you can be a praying parent. And you can show gratitude, speaking the truth in love, not in your strength but in God's strength in your family relationships as well. These have been, for me, the most important solutions in marriage, parenting, and family relationships.

The Truth

What is one thing you can begin to do today to lead your marriage or your family relationships in a better direction? Let's start with some Truth from God's Word.

> *Ephesians 1:16 AMPC I do not cease to give thanks for you, making mention of you in my prayers.*

> *Ephesians 4:15 AMP But speaking the truth in love in all things—both our speech and our lives expressing His truth, let us grow up in all things into Him following His example who is the Head—Christ.*

> *Philippians 2:13 AMP For it is not your strength, but it is God who is effectively at work in you, both to will and to work, that is, strengthening, energizing, and creating in you the longing and the ability to fulfill your purpose for His good pleasure.*

> *I Corinthians 13:4-8 ESV Love is patient and kind; love does not envy or boast; it is not arrogant or rude. It does not insist on its own way; it is not irritable or resentful; it does not rejoice at wrongdoing but rejoices with the truth. Love bears all things, believes all things, hopes all things, endures all things. Love never ends.*

Before You Ever Had The Problem,
God Had The Solution.

NOTES

Week Two – Day Five
Solutions For Leading Your Life
How Do You Lead In Your Work Or
Organization?

The Problem

Step one in leading your work or organization is to become someone worth following. As the saying goes, if you think you are a leader and look behind, but no one is following, you're just taking a hike. In today's marketplace, every company or organization needs good leadership. Our work and career are meant to be more than just a paycheck. It's even better to find meaning in your work as well as joy while you're making money. I think of the businessman in his nice suit talking to the guy dressed in rags on the park bench who seems to have hit a rough spot in his career, but he tells the business executive, "I'm actually wealthy beyond my wildest dreams! Unfortunately, my dreams were never very wild."

The problem comes when we are not committed to becoming a leader in the workplace worth following. If the essence of your influence and leadership in the workplace is trying to look impressive by walking around with your laptop open, covering your desktop computer with sticky notes that even you can't read, or using phrases like "Will this Scale?" in your meeting, just to look smart, then you need a better plan. As a side note, "Will this scale?" seems to be a good catchall phrase that drives people up the wall and may make you look smart, that is, until you must explain it. The leadership I am talking about is not impressing, manipulating, or controlling people but rather blessing them. Leading others well where we work is more about the influence that adds value rather than title or position. It's more about integrity and authenticity. It's also about leading by example more than telling others what to do. One of the great things about leadership, in general, is that anyone can learn leadership skills. Also, anyone can grow in their leadership, which means you can be on a new path starting today to lead better in your work or organization by being a leader others want to follow. Let's look at some solutions.

The Solution

I once read, "Making dreams happen doesn't only take money. It takes sweat." Something about that statement rings true, yet it is possibly the single biggest reason why people never lead well in their workplace. One of the secrets to leading in your workplace or organization isn't a secret at all. The secret? Hard work! Unfortunately, much of our perception of greatness hinges on the flawed idea of talent. But the truth is talent is never enough. In his excellent book "Outliers," Malcolm Gladwell calls it the 10,000-hour rule. He suggests the key to greatness in any field and the secret to influencing and leading others in that field is simply practice. 10,000 hours of it – or 20 hours a week for 10 years. The solution to leading where you work is truly built on the bedrock of an exceptional work ethic. It is important to note that hard work must be sustained to achieve this level of leadership influence. Just look at people who are considered at the top of their field, whether it be sports, arts, entertainment, technology, medicine, education, or whatever.

By and large, the elite are going at it for 15-20 years before hitting their zenith. (Okay, there are a few overnight successes, but they are the exception to the rule). You can be talented, smart, charming, and gifted, but if you are not willing to apply all of that to consistent, focused work, it won't matter. How often have you seen hard work overcome a lack of knowledge, talent, or skill? Or, as you will often hear after a championship game in almost any sport, how one team just "outworked" the other. By the same token, no combination of knowledge, talent, or skill can overcome a deficiency in work ethic. Do you want to rise above the rest, fulfill your call to be your best, and lead others in the process? Then, develop a great work ethic and keep at it! You can also try using more sports metaphors with your coworkers, like when something is great, say, "It's a home run." Tell them to "skate to where the puck will be and keep the ball rolling until you throw in the towel."

The Truth

What is one thing you can begin to do today to build a stronger work ethic in your life? Are you someone in your workplace, organization, or team who others choose to follow? What is it about you and the way you approach your work that makes you worth following? Let's start with some Truth from God's Word:

> *Colossians 3:23 ESV Whatever you do, work heartily, as for the Lord and not for men,*

> *Galatians 6:4-5 NLV Everyone should look at himself and see how he does his own work. Then he can be happy in what he has done. He should not compare*

himself with his neighbor. Everyone must do his own work.

Psalm 90:17 ESV Let the favor of the Lord our God be upon us, and establish the work of our hands upon us; yes, establish the work of our hands!

Proverbs 13:4 AMPC The appetite of the sluggard craves and gets nothing, but the appetite of the diligent is abundantly supplied.

Proverbs 14:23 CEV Hard work is worthwhile, but empty talk will make you poor.

Week Two – Day Six
Solutions For Leading Your Life
Why Does Your Leadership Legacy Matter?

The Problem

There was a sign posted in a small business that said;

"The 57 Rules of Success"
1. Deliver the Goods,
2. The other 56 don't matter.

There is something about leaving a successful legacy that matters. What does it take to achieve true success in life? I think one of the keys is intentional living. John C. Maxwell says intentional living is more important than where you were born, how much talent you have, or what kinds of connections you make. The problem is that most people simply don't live intentionally. They fly through life like their decisions don't matter and their days don't matter. It reminds me of the story of Muhammed Ali, who was on an airline flight once when the flight attendant came by doing her seat belt protocol, and before she could even say anything to him, he looked at her and said, "Superman, don't need no seatbelt." Her reply to him was, "Superman doesn't need no airplane, either. Buckle up, champ!" Like seatbelts matter in airplanes, today matters when it comes to leaving a legacy. People create a leadership legacy that matters by focusing on today. It may sound overly simplistic, but now is the only time you truly have since it's too late for yesterday, and tomorrow hasn't arrived. There are three specific problems or traps that lead to this legacy problem:

First, *we exaggerate yesterday.* This can be exaggerating the good *or* the bad. Some people never get over their past accomplishments or their negative experiences, and that shapes them for their entire lives. Good news: Yesterday ended last night!

Second, *we overestimate tomorrow.* Most people have a real hope-filled outlook for their future or expect things to worsen. But if they set their focus just on the future for better or worse, they miss the opportunity to start making it better today.

Third, *we underestimate today.* Have you ever heard someone say, "I'm just killing time," or "I'm just wasting the day away"? Benjamin Franklin said, "Time is the stuff life is made of." Yet many people let it slip through their fingers, never valuing its potential. Hoping for a good legacy in the future without investing in today is like a farmer waiting for a crop without ever planting any seed. That's a serious problem. Now, let's look at a solution.

The Solution

As I mentioned earlier, I think one of the keys to leaving a legacy that matters is intentional living. Intentional living is deliberate, not accidental. It demands thoughtful consideration, planning, and, well, intentionality. It is also a journey, not a destination. It is consistently requiring daily, weekly, and monthly follow-through. Intentional living is willful, meaning it is a choice. Despite obstacles, challenges, and distractions, it demands persistent effort. At this point, I've already lost some readers because this sounds like a lot of work, and you would be right to think so. However, the return on investment (ROI) for intentional living far outweighs the work it will take to make it a part of how you live. When it becomes your lifestyle, you have more than just good intentions. There is a significant difference between good intentions and intentional living. Simply cultivating good intentions without purposeful action can lead to frustration and unfulfillment. Let me show you three ways the power of intentional living can change your life.

1. Thinking Ahead:
The value of simply thinking ahead makes you more alert to the power of your choices to create a better future and a legacy that matters.

2. Making Every Day Count:
When you live intentionally, you recognize daily opportunities to make a difference and bless others.

3. Gradual Change for the Better:
You don't have to change everything at once. In fact, you can't. Intentional living encourages deliberate, consistent, and purposeful steps toward improvement.

Don't settle for good intentions when you can choose intentional living and make today matter for a better tomorrow.

The Truth

What is one thing you can begin to do today to lead your life more intentionally? Do you tend to over-exaggerate yesterday, underestimate today, or overestimate tomorrow? What would be a workable next step for you to take to avoid the traps of the legacy problem? It's always good to start with some Truth from God's Word to guide us to some of His solutions.

> *Matthew 6:33 NIV But seek first his kingdom and his righteousness, and all these things will be given to you as well.*

> *Ephesians 5:15-17 NIV "Be very careful, then, how you live—not as unwise but as wise, making the most of every opportunity, because the days are evil. Therefore, do not be foolish, but understand what the Lord's will is."*

> *Hebrews 10:35 AMP Do not, therefore, fling away your [fearless] confidence, for it has a glorious and great reward.*

Week Two – Day Seven
Solutions For Leading Your Life
Reflect, Record, Rejoice

Reflect

Look back over the past 6 days of devotionals and reflect on what stood out to you from what you read. Did you get any new insight? Any new understanding of God's word? Did you discover any areas of your life that you need some solutions?

Record

Write down your thoughts from what you just reflected on, putting down any impressions you received on paper or in digital format. Ask God to give you insight into what He wants to show you from what He has spoken to you this past week.

Rejoice

We should express words of thanksgiving and joy to God for His Word. Express thanksgiving and joy for His desire to speak to you, lead you, and give you solutions for living in faithful excellence. Make an intentional effort to find someone today with whom you can share what you learned from your time with God this week in these readings and, most of all, through His Truth!

Week Three – Day One
Solutions For Success
Simple Solutions For Significant Success

The Problem

Most people want to be successful. I don't think I can honestly say that I have met anyone who says they wake up in the morning thinking, "How can I fail or not succeed at something today?" Not that failure has to be fatal because sometimes we learn greatly from failure. I believe it was Henry Ford, a pioneer of automobile production, who said, "Failure is the opportunity to begin again more intelligently." Then there is one of my favorite failure quotes by Thomas Edison concerning the invention of the lightbulb when he states, "I have not failed. I've just found 10,000 ways that won't work."

There is something to be said for learning and persevering through failure, but let's talk about success. The first problem with success seems to be the definition. I'm not talking about Webster's dictionary definition or even the best leadership, personal development, or self-help definition you can find. What is *your* definition of success? How can you know if you ever reach success if you don't define it? It won't work as well for you to use my definition since your values, views, beliefs, and so forth may be different from mine. Even if you resort to the popular Google search default mode, the "definition" of success you will get is "The accomplishment of an aim or purpose." So, there you have it; you must have that "aim" or "purpose" defined to have success. Regarding something as significant as success in life, one would think that our definition, aim, and purpose would certainly be essential, if not critical!

The Solution

Over the next few days, we will look at "Solutions for Success in Life" and the starting point for the title of this book, "L.I.F.E. Leadership Solutions." I come back to this point because I believe you want *solutions for life* and *success*, or you wouldn't be reading this right now. This belief is based on my journey, my interaction with thousands of people over the several decades of ministry leadership, and as we will see in the following pages, through a fair amount of research and personal testimony. As we will find throughout this book, most solutions are not complicated, even solutions for something as complex as life. That is one of the trademarks of Jesus as He presented the Gospel. His message was simple and clear. People from every social class, ethnicity, and generation were drawn to His solutions for life. *"If any man wants to save his life, he must lose it."* (**Matthew 16:25**). I said it was simple, but it's not necessarily easy. The Sermon on the Mount in Matthew chapters 5-7 shows radical solutions for many areas of life. As the subtitle for this book states, "Before you ever had the problem, God had the solution." There is no better place to start than His solutions for success in life.

The Truth

Read the following passages and jot down your thoughts on what Jesus said about truth, life, and success.

John 3:32

John 8:36

John 10:10

John 14:6

Matthew 6:33

One of my life's sayings is this; "The greatest measure of my success is intimacy with Christ." This keeps it simple and attainable for me because Jesus has promised us that we will always be as close to Him (intimacy) as we desire to be. He has already made a way for this to happen for you and me through His death on the cross and His declared love for us. Plus, Jesus is continually showing me this is His desire. I believe God's plans for my success are directly tied to my decision to seek Him according to **Jeremiah 29:11-13 and Matthew 6:33**. He even goes on to say in **verse 14 of Jeremiah 29**, *"I will be found by you."* Jesus also encourages us that *"For everyone who asks, and keep on asking receives; and he who seeks and keep on seeking finds; and to him who knocks and keeps on knocking, the door shall be opened."* (**Luke 11:10** amp). So, what are you asking for and seeking after, and where are you knocking when it comes to solutions for success in life? I've included my personal definition of success on the last page of the appendix at the end of this book. It is my Life Mission Statement based on my core values.

Week Three – Day Two
Solutions For Success
What Are Some Definitions For Success?

The Problem

As I mentioned in the previous pages, there are many definitions for success in the world. Some good, some not-so-good, and some questionable. Some are extremely challenging, some are more easily achieved, and some are probably totally unattainable. There have been thousands of books written about "Success." Some of the ones with the word *success* in the title that grace my bookshelf are "The Success Principles" by Jack Canfield, "How Successful People Think" by John Maxwell, "Outliers; The Story of Success" by Malcolm Gladwell, "Predictable Success, "by Les McKeown and one of my all-time favorites, "Success is Not an Accident" by Tommy Newberry.

We'll return to Tommy Newberry's book in a minute, but I want you to think again about *your* definition of success. We're going to see that many success principles work for different areas, but life can be complex. So much of life is out of our control, and yet we still have the responsibility to make choices, determine a direction, or sit passively while life happens to us, not to mention how we respond to the things we can't control. Someone may be successful in their career while their family is falling apart. Maybe they climb their way to the top in some area of life and yet lose their values in the process. We have all read plenty of headlines about seemingly successful individuals whose lives came crashing down in a heap of a mess. So, what is the solution?

The Solution

Tommy Newberry is an author, speaker, and life coach who has earned the title "America's Success Coach." In his writings on success, he refers to three excellent principles to remember as we each determine our definition of success. The **first** one is *"Success is not an Accident."* This means there are intentional, deliberate steps taken to reach success in whatever goal or endeavor we choose. I don't know too many, if any, success stories where it just randomly happened. Even the person who wins the lottery takes the time to deliberately choose some numbers and buy a ticket. (By the way, I do not recommend playing the lottery as a plan for financial success).

The **second** principle is *"Success is about Stewardship."* This simply means that we have all been given specific talents, gifts, and abilities that, when discovered, developed, and exercised, will most likely lead to some success. We talked about this some back on Week One, Day Four. It's evident that some people have more natural talents, gifts, or abilities than others, but whatever amount you have, the level of success you will or will not see dramatically depends on how you steward (grow, develop, etc.) what has been given to you. This is where the world-class athletes separate themselves from the rest of us. It's where the elite musicians and artists, technicians and programmers, builders and creators, craftsmen and entrepreneurs in any field rise above the crowd to see greater success. The stewardship factor is also where someone with *less* natural talent, gifts, or abilities can surpass someone with greater amounts of those three resources simply because they worked harder to discover, develop, and grow them toward greater success. If you are a Biblical Christian, you also have "spiritual gifts," which bring a whole new level of potential for success. I like to say it and pray this way; "God has given me everything I need in body, soul and spirit, talent, gift and ability, resource and relationship, through Christ, to fulfill my mission!"

The **third** principle that Tommy Newberry refers to often and is one of his axioms is this; *"Your Success Blesses Others."* This one is frequently overlooked when talking about, thinking about, dreaming about, and working toward success in life. In truth, can it be considered a success if it does not bless others somehow? Referring to my life proverb of success that I mentioned earlier, "The greatest measure of my success is intimacy with Christ," I can see how that definition of success aligns with this principle. I know if I am growing and walking in intimacy with Jesus Christ, I will love my wife better. I will father and grandfather my kids and grandkids better, be a better friend, worker, leader, and more. My success in each of those endeavors truly does bless others. Think about those three simple principles, or as I like to call them, "pillars of success," as you continue to form your definition of success. It will be a good foundation on which to build. Now for the most important foundation, let's look at some Truth from God's Word.

The Truth

Read the following passages and jot down your thoughts on what the Bible says about stewardship, choices, talents, gifts, or abilities.

Before You Ever Had The Problem, God Had The Solution.

Matthew 25:14-30

Galatians 6:7-10

Proverbs 18:16

Romans 11:29

1 Corinthians 7:7

Week Three – Day Three
Solutions For Success
Is It Possible To Predict Success?

The Problem

So do you have *your* definition of success yet? I say "your definition" because it needs to be personal to you and something you believe in. It's okay if you are still working on it, as this is one of those critical life leadership solutions, and it takes some concentrated effort, so keep working. The good news is that there are some proven determinates and predictors of success in most areas of life. I hesitate to call them formulas but rather principles because there are always some potential wrinkles, hiccups, and unexpected or unplanned factors that affect outcomes. The problem is that most people either aren't aware of their definition of success or get sidetracked and discouraged in their efforts to pursue it. In my experience working with men, couples, students, families, and organizations I have heard almost every excuse out there. Some of the most famous people we know of who experienced great success also faced extreme challenges and obstacles. Just consider the following:

- **Albert Einstein was four years old before he could speak.**
- **Isaac Newton did poorly in grade school.**
- **Beethoven's music teacher once said of him, "As a composer, he is hopeless."**
- **When Thomas Edison was a boy, his teacher told him he was too stupid to learn anything.**

Before You Ever Had The Problem, God Had The Solution.

- **A newspaper editor fired Walt Disney because he had "no good ideas."**
- **Winston Churchill failed the 6th grade.**
- **Steven Spielberg dropped out of high school in his sophomore year. He was persuaded to come back and was placed in a learning-disabled class. He lasted a month and dropped out of school altogether.**

I don't think we'd consider any of these people a failure, though they each had some setbacks and failures. So, what allowed them to be successful even amidst struggles? The answer to that question may be less in what they did do and more in what they didn't do. That is where we will find today's solution.

The Solution

In his book, "No More Dreaded Mondays," Dan Miller outlines "5 Predictors of Success" that are seen time and time again in very successful people. Those predictors are *passion, determination, talent, self-discipline, and faith*. He further explains that these five characteristics have proven to carry more weight to achieving success than circumstances, luck, or good fortune. I would certainly agree with him in my own life experience as well as in the stories of so many others I have read about and known personally. For example, a person with **passion** has discovered how to tap into that intense emotional drive that goes beyond mere inspiration. Consider the stories of such innovators as Steve Jobs and his driving passion for putting "a computer on every desk in every home." It seemed unheard of and impossible by most people at the time.

When I think about **determination**, I think about one of my wife's favorite entertainers, Dolly Parton. She was laughed at by those in attendance at her High School graduation when she announced she was "going to Nashville to be a star" for her future plans. She would certainly need some determination to reach that dream as she had grown up in poverty as the fourth of twelve children and would face even more hardships along the way. In her own words, the crowd's response that day at her graduation would prove to be one of her greatest motivations to fuel her **determination**.

This "unlikely success story" went on to write over 3,000 songs, eventually holding the record for the number of awards for a female artist, including 7 Grammys and an Emmy. She ultimately became a business mogul, opening the Dollywood Theme Park in Pigeon Forge, Tennessee. As a philanthropist, her "Imagination Library" program was adopted in 600 communities throughout 41 states. I would say *determination* served her well. She would certainly be a person who had all the other five predictors moving her forward to incredible success in life. **"Determination,"** committed; **"Passion,"** no doubt; **"Talent,"** proven; **"Self-discipline,"** abundant; and **"Faith,"** a foundation of her life according to her testimony.

So, how evident are these five critical characteristics in your life? Does Jesus and the Bible have anything to say about them and their importance? Let's look at each one and see how building the truth of God's word in our lives moves us towards success that matters.

The Truth

Before You Ever Had The Problem,
God Had The Solution.

Read the following passages and jot down your thoughts on what the Bible says.

Passion: Matthew 6:21; Romans 12:11

Determination: 1 Corinthians 15:58; Hebrews 12:1-3; Philippians 4:13

Talent: Exodus 35:10; Proverbs 22:29; Romans 12:6-8

Self-Discipline: 2 Timothy 1:7; 1 Thessalonians 5:8

Faith: Matthew 17:20; Hebrews 11:1, 6

Consider how each of these five areas would be a benefit or catalyst as you pursue your definition of success. Ask God today to show you where He would have you develop at least one characteristic as you pursue His purposes and success that matters for your life.

Week Three – Day Four
Solutions For Success
Developing Five Essentials Of Success

The Problem

Successful leadership is defined as "vision combined with the resolve, courage, and endurance it takes to complete a goal or mission." When I was a student at the University of Georgia (Go Dawgs!), my Campus Crusade for Christ Ministry Director used to say there are three kinds of people in the world – 1) Those who make things happen, 2) those who watch things happen and 3) those who say, "what happened?"

The problem we're discussing today is often described as inertia, moving forward, taking action, etc. It's also about sustaining that action, as well as fueling the power of that movement. Sometimes "sustainability" is the most vital "ability" we need. Therefore, one of the problems for success in any endeavor is the failure to move forward with purpose, passion, and perseverance.

Many who never see the potential victories or the success in life they desire often spend their life only dreaming about the day their "big break" will come. This is not the pathway to take as it is filled with unnecessary delays and distractions rather than clear vision and goals. Again, the solution is simple but not easy. The enemy called "easy" has kept some of the most gifted people I know from achieving their desired purpose due to not having the resolve, courage, and endurance to overcome the problems that come their way. The truth is adversity can help us to focus more, eliminating the non-essentials and devoting ourselves to what is truly important.

Here is a critical L.I.F.E. Leadership Solution – If you're going to fulfill your purpose, you must first determine to go to the one true source for the courage to stay the course and persevere for the prize. That source is Jesus Christ as we place our faith, hope, and confidence in Him! As Rick Warren, author and former Senior Pastor of Saddleback Church, says, "Fear is a self-imposed prison that will keep you from becoming what God intends for you to be. Fear may be where you are now, but faith is what you could be."

Speaking of real-life solutions, I recently read some excellent advice from that famous Oklahoma cowboy, Mr. Will Rogers: "Never Slap a man who's chewing tobacco, never miss a good chance to shut up, and always drink upstream from the herd." He also said to "never forget that good judgment comes from experience and a lot of that comes from bad judgment." (I've seen that one a few times in my life) But I digress.

The Solution

In his book, "Leadership, The Power of a Creative Life," Rick Joyner outlines "5 Essentials of Success" that are present in the lives of most successful people:

1. **They define their goal.**
2. **They stay focused on their goal.**

3. **They have the wisdom and resolve to gather the necessary resources or training to accomplish their goal.**
4. **They do not associate with "problem-oriented people" but surround themselves with "solution-oriented people."**
5. **They refuse to let obstacles stop them or change their course.**

Rather than extensively unpacking or going into detail concerning these five essentials, I strongly encourage you to read his book. The first five chapters alone (only 45 pages) are worth the entire book price. It's filled with surprisingly simple steps and solutions for success in any endeavor. I have personally applied these essentials in my own life to reach some big goals, and I have seen them applied in the lives of others I have worked with to help them start businesses, launch ministries, and make significant life decisions. One guy I know used these five essentials to find the love of his life, and they are now over ten years happily married with two kids!

Yet, as with any worthwhile endeavor, dream, or goal, there is a demand to leave comfort and security behind as "faith" is often spelled R-I-S-K." For example, why is it that many who have the talent to become a great musician or athlete instead settle for spending their life watching others perform? What is the dividing line between living a faith-filled, fruitful life rather than a life of mediocrity, fear, and frustration? One thing is for sure: the best pianist to play started poorly. The best pitcher to ever pitch in baseball did not throw a 95-mph fastball when he threw his first pitch. I like the story of the world's foremost cellist, Pablo Casals, who, at 83 years of age, was asked why he continued to practice four and five hours a day. Casals answered, "Because I think I am making progress." That is the mentality and attitude represented in the "Five Essentials for Success." You must determine that you are in it for the long haul to go the distance.

Fulfilling any worthwhile dream or goal will be more of a marathon than a sprint. Unless your goal is to be the fastest sprinter in the world, then yes, it would be a sprint. This brings up another piece of advice from Will Rogers; "If you find yourself in a hole, stop digging." I like the way he keeps it simple!

The Truth

Read the following passages and jot down your thoughts on what the Bible says about them.

Vision: Proverbs 29:11; Ephesians 2:10

Goals: 1 Corinthians 9:24; 2 Corinthians 5:9

Courage: Psalm 27:1; 31:24; Deuteronomy 31:6

Perseverance: James 1: 4-5,12; Galatians 6:9

Purpose: Psalm 138:8; Romans 8:28; 2 Thessalonians 1:11

Consider how you might apply one or more of these five essentials for a goal dream you have in your heart. Ask God today to stir up within you a passion for persevering, stepping out, and following through on one of these essentials. Then go after the success that you believe genuinely matters most!

Before You Ever Had The Problem,
God Had The Solution.

NOTES

Week Three – Day Five
Solutions For Success
A Present Solution For Your Future Success

The Problem

Success is a planned outcome, not an accident. One of the reasons success and failure are both predictable is because they follow the Law of Sowing and Reaping. Simply stated, if you want to reap more *good* fruit, you must sow more *good* seed. Success in life is not based on what you need to do but on what seeds you are planting. It's an essential fact of life that many fail to understand, much less apply this essential truth for the life they want to live.

It is essentially impossible to harvest something that has not been sown, though many squander their entire lives attempting to do just this only to end up in frustration. Both right thinking and right actions increase greater success. Success, and failure for that matter, are not based on coincidence but on consequences. If you want to know what seeds you planted in the past, look around and see what you're reaping today. One of the marks of a person progressing toward Christlikeness is the acceptance of complete responsibility for one's life. When you accept total responsibility, you recognize that you are the source of all your choices, decisions, and actions.

The Solution

Before You Ever Had The Problem, God Had The Solution.

The reason this law of sowing and reaping is so critical is that everything you do or fail to do counts. Every action has a consequence, even if it isn't immediate. At this moment, you are becoming more like the person you want to become, or you are not! There is no neutrality. An extraordinary life is simply the accumulation of thousands of extraordinary choices, often unseen by others and known only to you and God. This is why we need our minds renewed daily, our thoughts set on Christ, our mission clear, and our goals (action steps) worthwhile and compelling.

I mentioned author Tommy Newberry earlier, and in his excellent book *"Success Is Not An Accident,"* he puts it this way.

> *"You are rich with choice, and your choices reveal who you really are. More than any other single factor, you are where you are today because of the choices you have made. You've made decisions about what to learn and what not to learn. You have made decisions about who to spend your time with and who not to spend your time with. You've made decisions to believe some things and not to believe others. You made decisions about who you would date, who you married, and whether you will have children. You've made decisions to persevere and decisions to give up. You can choose to plant the seeds of the spirit so that you will see more of the "fruit of the spirit."*

This is great news. Or it *can be* that at any moment, we can choose to make a different or better choice that moves us in a different direction. It may even be a "defining moment choice" that moves you toward the purpose and destiny God has for you! You can choose to say "no" to the lesser things so you can say "yes" to the better things. You've decided either to write down exciting life goals or just wing them. You have made decisions to give in to fear or decisions to press on in the face of fear. You've decided to be the best or act like all the rest. Consider for a moment all your decisions in just the last three years. These choices are made daily, hourly, and minute-to-minute. Imagine having made a different choice in some key area. How might your life be different today?"

The Truth

It can be summed up in this simple truth. *We are always only one decision away from a totally different life – for better or for worse!*

As you consider this simple L.I.F.E. Leadership Solution, jot down your thoughts on what the following verses say about renewing our minds, being intentional about where we set our minds, and the seed we choose to plant for the fruit we want to see.

John 15:4-7

Galatians 6:7-9

Romans 12:1-2

Before You Ever Had The Problem, God Had The Solution.

Colossians 3:1-2

Proverbs 23:7

Week Three – Day Six
Solutions For Success
Four Pillars To Build On For Success

The Problem

What happens when you build on a poor foundation? Well, we can look at the Leaning Tower of Pisa to get a good idea. It was famously titled for the wrong reason. An even better example would be the "Parable of the Two Builders" from **Matthew 7:24-27**. The winds and storms of life beat down on both houses, resulting in the house being built on sandy land crumbling while the house being built on a firm foundation ("the words of Jesus," as He explains it) standing firm. That would be considered a "successful" structure, and so it goes with any success plan. A good foundation is essential to a good outcome.

One of the most enjoyable things I did with my two sons when they were growing up was to create several experiences based on some ideas from a book by Robert Lewis titled, "Raising a Modern Day Knight – a Father's Role in Guiding His Son to Authentic Manhood" (1997, Focus on the Family Publishing). In his book, Mr. Lewis describes what he calls "a vision for manhood" and offers four basic ideas to impart this vision. They are:

1. **Reject Passivity**
2. **Accept Responsibility**
3. **Lead Courageously**
4. **Live for the Greater Reward**

Before You Ever Had The Problem, God Had The Solution.

We had fun as we developed experiences with these principles and this knighthood theme, doing devotionals and books together, creating heraldry shields, and going to Medieval Times on each of their 12th birthdays. We had some other fun events all centered around this vision for manhood. These four principles have also been a personal focus and prayer for my life over the years as I view each as a catalyst for success in various areas of life. I would suggest that these four pillars of success are worthwhile guidelines to build on for both men and women.

Let's look at each of these principles in more detail today as I have seen them to be trustworthy leadership solutions to problems that many individuals face. Consider the destructive power of *passivity*. It seems to lull us to sleep and paralyze us from moving forward in life. What about the problem of failing to *accept responsibility*? This has become a significant issue in our culture today. Almost anyone can see the tremendous need for *courageous leadership* on many levels in our society. As we consider what it means to *live for the greater reward*, that simply starts with the self-discipline to determine to live with a delayed gratification mindset. It's a belief that the prize is worth the sacrifice it takes to attain it. Thomas Edison famously said, "Opportunity is missed by most people because it is dressed in overalls and looks like work." These four pillars provide an excellent foundation for building your life leadership but require work to implement them effectively.

The Solution

When you are anchored in the reality of responsibility, you are far more likely to act in ways that will not later become causes of regret, frustration, or embarrassment. Life is a two-for-one deal. With every choice, you get a free consequence. This is the mindset and the attitude of one who conquers in life. Are you ready to slay the "Dragon of Passivity"? It will require you to take responsibility for your life, your choices, and the direction you determine to go. It will take courageous faith to overcome obstacles, oppositions, and setbacks. It will call you to live for the greater reward – this is an eternal mindset with a view of the prize.

My challenge to you in this L.I.F.E. Leadership solution today is for you to *"live as you will have wished to have lived when you are dying."* (Christian Gellert) This one quality alone will set you apart from 99% of the rest of the world. What you and I do today and every day matters because each day matters. It is *"the Day that the Lord has made, we will rejoice and be glad in it."* (**Psalm 118:24** AMP) It's a 24-hour segment of time never lived before and never to be lived again. You may never live to see another day like this one. You may never be closer to a decision you need to make, a step you need to take, a sin you need to forsake, or a greater understanding of what's at stake. This is one reason why your core values, personal mission, and definition of success are essential. However, your core values don't mean much if they're not your core convictions and determining factors for how you live each day. This is what it takes to *Lead Courageously* – in any area of your life.

The Truth

Before You Ever Had The Problem, God Had The Solution.

Take a few minutes to jot down what God may be saying to you through the following verses, which relate to the four principles mentioned earlier.

Reject Passivity: I Corinthians 16:13; 2 Timothy 1:7

Accept Responsibility: Matthew 25:21; 1 Corinthians 9:24

Lead Courageously: Joshua 1:1-9; Matthew 16:24-25

Live for the Greater Reward: Matthew 16:25-26; Hebrews 10:35-36

Tomorrow, you will have the opportunity to take a few minutes to reflect on this past week and write down any thoughts, impressions, takeaways, and, most notably, any action steps based on what you have read this week. This is an essential action step you can take for your personal growth. The most significant change in our lives usually comes from intentional choices we make that facilitate that growth. Let me encourage you that if you genuinely want to see growth in any area, it is always possible by God's grace and your desire to do your part. I tell myself this: I'm not going to get where I *want* to be (or *need* to be) if I *won't* do what I *need* to do to get there." Let's go!

Before You Ever Had The Problem,
God Had The Solution.

NOTES

Week Three – Day Seven
Solutions For Success
Reflect, Record, Rejoice

Reflect

Look back over the past 6 days of devotionals and reflect on what stood out to you from what you read. Did you get any new insight? Any new understanding of God's word? Did you discover any areas of your life that you need some solutions?

Record

Write down your thoughts from what you just reflected on, putting down any impressions you received on paper or in digital format. Ask God to give you insight into what He wants to show you from what He has spoken to you this past week.

Rejoice

You should take the time to express thanksgiving and joy to God for His Word, for His desire to speak to you, lead you, and give you solutions for living in faithful excellence. Make an intentional effort to find someone today with whom

Before You Ever Had The Problem, God Had The Solution.

you can share what you learned from your time with God this week in these readings and, most of all, through His Truth!

Week Four – Day One
Solutions From Five Faithful Friends
Not How, But WHO

The Problem

"The greatest mistake we make is living in constant fear that we will make one." - John Maxwell. Now, that is a problem that applies to many areas of life. It's been proven that if a basketball player focuses more on missing the shot than hitting it, he will be more likely to miss it. What we believe truly matters. What you tell yourself repeatedly really matters. In his book, "The Power of the Subconscious Mind," Dr. Joseph Murphy says, "Your subconscious mind does not argue with you. It accepts what your conscious mind decrees."

That is another reason why it is so important to consistently confess the truth of God's word over our lives. Most people have beliefs that limit their possibilities and paralyze their progress, which results in working against God's work in their lives. But this does not have to be your story. It may be beliefs about their capabilities, how people view them, or past experiences that have negatively shaped them. However, moving beyond these limiting beliefs is the first step to becoming who God has called you to be. It takes courage, humility, and intentionality to identify limiting beliefs and then replace them with the truth of what God says.

The Solution

Before You Ever Had The Problem, God Had The Solution.

When I think of this personal leadership solution, the Old Testament character Gideon comes to mind. (Judges 6:11-24) He had so many limiting beliefs he would have probably been the last person picked to deliver Israel from an enemy. He saw himself as a weakling and a nobody from a nothing family. He was discouraged, doubting, and so fearful that he hid in a wine press while threshing wheat. The story itself is sort of humorous. However, God's Word for Gideon (the Truth) totally transcended his limiting beliefs. From these verses, we see truth and victory.

- **The Lord is with you (6:12)**
- **You are a mighty man of fearless courage (6:12)**
- **Go in your might from God (6:14)**
- **You will save Israel from Midian (6:14)**
- **I (God) have sent you (6:14)**
- **Surely I (GOD) will be with you (6:14)**
- **Peace be to you, do not fear (6:23)**

Anytime we make the 'mind-shift" from limiting beliefs to God's transcending Truth, we experience a decisive breakthrough. This was true for Gideon, and it is true for you and me. The shift to believing the truth, confessing it, and acting on it will mean the difference from "what I could have done" regrets to seeing "**Mark 10:27** With God, all things are possible" living.

It will always be more about the "Who" in you than anything in your strength or ability. **Philippians 2:13** reminds us it is *"Not in your own strength for it is God Who is all the while effectually at work in you, energizing and creating in you the power and desire, both to will and to work for His good pleasure and satisfaction and delight."* Wow, just soak in that truth for a minute and allow God's possibilities to speak to your personal life, relationships, job, career, or future!

As mentioned earlier, you have tremendous power to choose where you lead your thoughts and set your mind. When you are intentional about this one area, you will plant seeds that produce the best fruit available. Take responsibility from this day forward to lead your life by the power and truth of Christ in you, the "Who" that makes everything possible!

The Truth

Do you remember this simple truth? *We are always only one decision away from a totally different life – for better or for worse!* Is there a truth decision you need to make today about the "who in you"?

As you consider this simple leadership reality, jot down your thoughts on what the following verses say about the "Who" in you. Also, we must continue to be intentional about where we set our minds as well as the seed we choose to plant for the fruit we want to see.

> *Mark 10:27 NKJV But Jesus looked at them and said, "With men it is impossible, but not with God; for with God all things are possible."*

> *Philippians 2:13 AMPC Not in your own strength] for it is God Who is all the while effectually at work in you energizing and creating in you the power and desire, both to will and to work for His good pleasure and satisfaction and delight.*

Before You Ever Had The Problem,
God Had The Solution.

Philippians 4:13 NKJV I can do all things through Christ who strengthens me.

Week Four – Day Two
Solutions From Five Faithful Friends
Know The WHAT And Find The WIN

The Problem

Have you ever been to "GYBIG Boot Camp"? Have you ever even heard of it? Maybe it's time to go for a week, a month, or even a year. "GYBIG" stands for "Get Your Butt In Gear." It's a reality check and a wake-up call that time is running out. Maybe you have been putting something off for too many days, using too many excuses when you just need to coach yourself to GYBIG! Listen, I've been there plenty of times, and it has proven to be an effective boot camp. It's a reminder that the process (the daily steps to your goal or dream) is part of the price required to obtain the prize.

Procrastination is a nasty problem to face, but one way you can overcome it is to keep your eyes on the prize. Roger Bannister was a great track athlete who broke the four-minute mile barrier in 1954. Even doctors said running the mile in under four minutes was physically impossible. But Bannister did it – and as soon as he did, other runners quickly began breaking his record. When Bannister proved running that fast was not impossible, it became apparent that the real barrier had been psychological, not physical. To this day, Bannister's record has been beaten by over 16 seconds! That would actually put Bannister over a football field behind the fastest runner in a mile race as they cross the finish line. The Roman

Before You Ever Had The Problem, God Had The Solution.

Emperor Marcus Aurelius was quoted as saying, "Because a thing seems difficult for you, do not think it impossible for anyone to accomplish." So, is the "What" the problem or the solution, or maybe both? Let's see.

The Solution

In the past, there have been so many things thought impossible, such as airplanes, television, heart transplants, the moon landing, personal computers, and even that cell phone you're attached to that is more powerful than the first computers. To people living only 150 years ago, these would have seemed like magic or miracles. So how do you achieve the impossible "what"? Here is an interesting thing about the word "impossible" from my friend, the late Ed DeCosta; "Inside the word impossible, you'll find two words – I'm possible!" When you look at it that way, it makes many things look even more possible. Like the lyrics to the classic Billie Holiday song, "Crazy He Calls Me."

The difficult I'll do right now, the impossible may take a little while.

When you find and define your "what," you can find and define your "win." For Roger Bannister, it was running the fastest mile he could, which at the time became the fastest mile ever, which before seemed impossible. One key often overlooked in pursuing seemingly impossible dreams is patient endurance or, as some refer to it, steadfastness. The constant effort to keep working at it and stay focused on the prize is a challenge. As the saying goes, "Rome wasn't built in a day" (that's not in the Bible, by the way, but it is true), and it took a few years to get to the moon. It also took President

John F. Kennedy to issue this major challenge – what is often called a BHAG (Big Hairy Audacious Goal) – to our rocket boys. The moon *was* the WIN! Again, I think of another classic standard, "Fly me to the Moon," and the saying, "Shoot for the moon, and if you miss, you'll still be among the stars."

Do you have one of those BHAGs in your life? Something that seems impossible, certainly not possible without God's hand on it. I challenge you to identify an "impossible what" for your own life and BHAG and make it your WIN. That win stands for "What's Important Now." It could be as big as coming up with some innovative idea that impacts thousands of lives or as little as deciding to go to GYBIG Boot Camp for a few weeks to make some needed changes in your life. Hey, a win is a WIN! So, the "what" is essential, but don't forget about the "when." That is the faithful friend we will talk about tomorrow.

The Truth

I'm thinking of one more classic standard, sung best by the original artist, Louis Armstrong, "What a Wonderful World." The lyrics in the third verse say, "I hear babies cry, I watch them grow, they'll learn much more than I'll ever know. And I think to myself, what a wonderful world." Consider the following verses as you dream of the wonderful future God has for you while you consider His possibilities for your "impossible what."

> *Luke 18:27 NKJV But He said, "The things which are impossible with men are possible with God."*

Before You Ever Had The Problem, God Had The Solution.

Ephesians 3:20 ESV Now to him who is able to do far more abundantly than all that we ask or think, according to the power at work within us,

Week Four – Day Three
Solutions From Five Faithful Friends
If Not Now, Then When?

The Problem

Have you ever had a deadline and knew you would never make it? It makes sense that they call it a "dead"-line," since you may have felt like you would be dead if you didn't make it. As Calvin in the comic strip "Calvin and Hobbes" quipped, "God put me on earth to accomplish certain things. Right now, I am so far behind, I'll never die." *"When"* can be a real problem if you never state it. You inevitably find yourself constantly on the road to someday, which always leads to nowhere. Even as great as goal setting is, especially the BHAG (big hairy audacious goal) kind, it probably won't happen without a "when," a deadline, or a due date. Author and executive coach Ed DeCosta put it this way.

> *"A Dream written down with a date becomes a*
> *goal.*
> *A Goal broken down into steps becomes a plan.*
> *A Plan backed by action makes your dreams come*
> *true!"*

The way we unleash the power of growth goals, whether spiritual, physical, mental, or any area, is to give yourself a specific time and date to see it accomplished. One day is really a non-day. "Maybe later" is not a good mindset or attitude if you want to change your life, do something that makes a difference, or become a better you who blesses others. So how do we tackle the "when" problem if, as we have already seen, "when" is also the solution?

The Solution

The first clue to getting to the "when" is to get to that special place where you know now is the time. Resistance to change is universal, so if that is one of your obstacles, you are in good company. Of course, you don't want to be as extreme as one of the 1600 International Flat Earth Society members of America. Their president, Charles K. Johnson, testifies, "When I saw the globe in grade school, I didn't accept it then, and I don't accept it now." The truth is people do not resist change as much as they resist being changed. It seems that before anything positive can change around you, there must first be a change inside you. Think of it this way. The distance between where you stand right now and where you want to be is measured by the changes you are willing to make in your life. John Maxwell, author and leadership expert, says this is about the power of when.

1. **People change *when* they *hurt* enough that they *have to* change.**
2. **People change *when* they *learn* enough that they *want to* change.**
3. **People change *when* they *receive* enough that they *are able to* change.**

A great example is the Swedish Chemist Alfred Nobel, who made a fortune by inventing dynamite and other powerful explosives that drive weapons of mass destruction. Ironically, they named the "Nobel *Peace* Prize" after him. But the rest of the story is the best of the story, and it goes like this:

When Alfred's brother died years earlier before his Peace Prize notoriety, the newspaper obituary was mistakenly written about Alfred and described him as someone "who made it possible to kill more people, more quickly than anyone in history." Reading that was when Alfred Nobel decided to change his legacy and, for the rest of his life, devoted most of his wealth towards efforts that benefit others, not destroy them. It was a defining moment, but he still had to decide *when* to *change* the narrative of how he would be remembered. It's good to remember that it's never too late to change, and you have the power to start it in you. So, when will you start if this is the solution for the change you want to see? As the saying goes, if not now, when?

The Truth

Take a few minutes to pray through the following verses and consider what God may say to you about your "when." Do you hurt enough that you know you must change? Have you learned enough that you want to change? Have you received enough that you are able to change? There is truly no significant growth without change. The "when" is your friend!

> II Corinthians 5:17 NKJV Therefore, if anyone is in Christ, he is a new creation; old things have passed away; behold, all things have become new.

> Isaiah 43:19 AMPC Behold, I am doing a new thing! Now it springs forth; do you not perceive and know it and will you not give heed to it? I will even make a way in the wilderness and rivers in the desert.

Before You Ever Had The Problem, God Had The Solution.

Romans 12:2 NIV Do not conform to the pattern of this world, but be transformed by the renewing of your mind. Then you will be able to test and approve what God's will is—his good, pleasing and perfect will.

Week Four – Day Four
Solutions From Five Faithful Friends
The Road To Someday Leads To Nowhere

The Problem

Are you a Nowhere Man? Or Nowhere Woman? I'm going back to 1965 and a song the Beatles made famous titled "Nowhere Man." The lyrics say, "He's a real nowhere man, living in a nowhere land, living out his nowhere plan for nobody. Doesn't have a point of view, knows not where he's going to, isn't he a bit like you and me." I hope that is not you, as it sounds pretty bleak to me.

The problem is that so much of life can pull us to becoming aimless, never moving forward and essentially going nowhere. A nowhere man gets caught in the drift of apathy and no direction for life. This drift I am referring to is subtle and quite dangerous. It can easily lead to a life of regret if you fail to deal with it. The drift starts with a distraction, which can be defined as an attraction to a non-priority. Distractions of the "nowhere man" kind are momentum killers, passion stealers, and enthusiasm crushers. I don't know many people who wake up in the morning and say, "Today, I plan to be distracted." Yet many individuals go nowhere forward with their lives, stuck in the same regrets and disappointments, "living out a nowhere plan for nobody." What is the solution to avoiding this "nowhere man" trap and instead finding ways to fuel your life with passion and enthusiasm? Once again, I am glad you asked, so let's look at one today.

The Solution

Do you desire more direction, passion, and enthusiasm in your life? Passion comes from within you, providing enthusiasm, focus, and energy. The word enthusiasm comes from the Greek word "entheos," which means "to be filled with God." So, when you are filled with the spirit of God, you become supernaturally inspired and passionate. This type of passion can express itself dynamically and energetically at times. Other times, it expresses itself more peacefully and calmly, like Mother Teresa's passion for ministering to the needs of the dying in Calcutta. You may have seen both types and find yourself more like one or the other. There is that person who can't wait to get up in the morning, eager and energetic. They are filled with purpose, committed to their mission, and not hesitant to let you know about it. They are called "vegans." (Just kidding) Seriously though, when true passion and enthusiasm are engaged, you find your life more enjoyable in many ways. You get more clarity about where you want to go and how to get there. Here are three solutions I have found to get out of nowhere land and into a life that matters.

1. **Wake Up:**

Romans 13:11-12 AMPC says, "This a critical hour, and it is time to rouse to reality." Don't take this drift lightly, and face reality. We are encouraged to put some urgency behind the decision to "Fling away the works and deeds of darkness and put on the full armor of light." That sounds like a clear direction to me!

2. Rise Up:

Isaiah 60:1 AMPC encourages us to "Arise from the depression and prostration in which circumstances have kept you. Arise to a new life!" No matter what the circumstances, we can choose to rise up. Why? Because we have resurrection power available to us through Jesus Christ. It goes on to say, "For your light has come, and the glory of the Lord has risen upon you!" That is all the power you need to rise up.

3. Fire Up:

Romans 12:11-12 ESV Do not be slothful in zeal, be fervent in spirit, serve the Lord. 12 Rejoice in hope, be patient in tribulation, be constant in prayer.

That certainly can get me fired up and stay fired up as I focus on Him. God's fire in us sets us ablaze and keeps us from the tendency to drift!

The Truth

Take a few minutes to pray through the following verses and consider what God may say to you about your "where." Whatever your where may be, you will get there better when you wake up, rise up, and fire up with God's Word! Here are a few reminders and a great place to start.

Isaiah 60:1 AMPC ARISE from the depression and prostration in which circumstances have kept you—rise to a new life! Shine, be radiant with the glory of the Lord, for your light has come, and the glory of the Lord has risen upon you!

Romans 12:11-12 AMP "Never lagging behind in diligence; aglow in the Spirit, enthusiastically serving the Lord; constantly rejoicing in hope because of our confidence in Christ, steadfast and patient in distress, devoted to prayer, continually seeking wisdom, guidance and strength."

Romans 13:11-12 AMP Do this, knowing that this is a critical time. It is already the hour for you to awaken from your sleep of spiritual complacency; for our salvation is nearer to us now than when we first believed in Christ. 12) The night of this present evil age is almost gone and the day of Christ's return is almost here. So let us fling away the works of darkness and put on the full armor of light.

Week Four – Day Five
Solutions From Five Faithful Friends
Seeing Beyond The How

The Problem

Seeing beyond the **how** can become problematic if you label yourself too young or too old. Is there really some perfect age you must be to succeed in life, make a difference, or achieve some sort of greatness? If you think you're too young, you might think you don't have enough experience, or you don't have the right college degree, or you may worry about what others think about you. If you believe you are too old, you might think you didn't start soon enough, it's too late for you, or some other limiting mindset. Let's just crush that lie immediately with this bit of truth; "You're never too late to become who you might have been."

Most people are limited by their logic, but logic can be a dream stealer. If you look at your life circumstances and options only from a human point of view – your age, connections, experience, and resources – you may miss the purposes God has put in your heart that supersede human logic. All your logic says, "There's no way, it's too big, I'm too small, I don't have enough _____, it's never happened for anyone in my family, etc." Here's the question: Are you going to let your logic and human reasoning determine your future and what you can only see to set the limits on your life? Or will you let what God says about you and His plans for you determine your future and what is possible? Experience alone can be overrated. After all, for some reason, it seems experience is something you don't get until just after you need it. There is a better solution, so let's dig in to see if we can find it.

The Solution

To see beyond the "how," you have to choose to rise higher, move past your ground-level perspective, and get to a higher view. First, what others think about you is none of your business. Getting that mindset will save you all sorts of worry, anxiety, and general frustration. Maybe you've heard of Dr. Daniel Amen's 18/40/60 Rule: When you're 18, you worry about what everybody is thinking of you; when you're 40, you don't care what anybody thinks of you; when you're 60, you realize nobody's been thinking about you at all. Surprise, surprise! Most people are too busy worrying about their own lives, and if they are thinking about you, they are wondering what you are thinking about them. You probably want a better view of life than that perspective. The solution is to understand that your age is only a number. If you're still saying I'm just too young to do whatever, then consider the following:

1. **David was supposedly *too young* to slay a giant.**
2. **Shadrach, Meshach, and Abednego were *too young* to stand against a King and his empire for their faith.**
3. **Mary was *too young* to be the mother of the Messiah.**
4. **The boy with the five loaves and two fish was *too young* to be used by Jesus to provide lunch for over 5 thousand people!**

As 1 Timothy 4:12 says, "Let no one think less of you because of your youth, but be an example to them in speech, conduct, love, faith, and purity." The list of others in the "too young" camp who have done incredible exploits is both numerous and amazing. Make sure your "God-image" is correct, and you'll have a better "self-image."

If you're still saying you're too old, look no further than a couple of Biblical heroes by the name of Joshua and Caleb. These two guys were certainly up in years when taking the Promised Land and overcoming massive obstacles. The epic passage from Joshua 1:1-9 takes place when Joshua was in his 70's. Then, consider that Caleb was 85 when he was commissioned to take the hill country and conquer the Anakim (giant people) from Hebron. This is one octogenarian who wasn't too old for his calling and mission!

Even in recent years, you have J.R.R. Tolkien, who was 63 when the third book of "The Lord of the Rings" trilogy was finally published. Others like Julia Child, the famous TV chef who didn't even learn to cook until she was almost 40 and didn't start her award-winning TV show until she was 51. One of my favorites was Susan Boyle, the 48-year-old unknown amateur singer discovered in 2009 when she performed "I Dreamed a Dream" from the musical "Les Misérables" on the TV show, "Britain's Got Talent." From there, she skyrocketed to the tune of 5 albums, 19 million copies sold, two Grammy nominations, and a net worth of $37 million. I would say whatever dream she dreamed came true! If you're still breathing, God's not done with you yet! But it requires action on your part, and that is where you need the "Why" that we will talk about tomorrow.

Before You Ever Had The Problem, God Had The Solution.

The Truth

Take a few minutes to pray through the following verses and consider how you may be limiting yourself by not seeing past the "how." Whether you think you're too young or too old, none of that really matters.

1 Timothy 4:12 NIV Don't let anyone look down on you because you are young, but set an example for the believers in speech, in conduct, in love, in faith and in purity.

Exodus 7:7 NIV Moses was eighty years old and Aaron eighty-three when they spoke to Pharaoh.

1 Samuel 17:33 NIV Saul replied, "You are not able to go out against this Philistine and fight him; you are only a young man, and he has been a warrior from his youth."

Joshua 14:10-12 NKJV (Caleb speaking) And now, behold, the Lord has kept me alive, as He said, these forty-five years, ever since the Lord spoke this word to Moses while Israel wandered in the wilderness; and now, here I am this day, eighty-five years old. Yet I am as strong this day as on the day that Moses sent me; just as my strength was then, so now is my strength for war, both for going out and for coming in. Now therefore, give me this mountain of which the Lord spoke in that day; for you heard in that day how the Anakim (descendants of Goliath) were there, and that the cities were great and fortified. It may be that the Lord will be with me, and I shall be able to drive them out as the Lord said.

Jeremiah 1:6-8 ESV Then I said, "Ah, Lord God ! Behold, I do not know how to speak, for I am only a youth." But the Lord said to me, "Do not say, 'I am only a youth'; for to all to whom I send you, you shall go, and whatever I command you, you shall speak. Do not be afraid of them, for I am with you to deliver you, declares the Lord."

Before You Ever Had The Problem,
God Had The Solution.

NOTES

Week Four – Day Six
Solutions From Five Faithful Friends
How Big Is Your Why?

The Problem

There is a universal truth in life that says, "How you do *anything* is how you do *everything*." It may sound a bit simplistic, but it does play out rather consistently. It's important to consider when asking the question, "How do I get from where I am to where I want to be?" The problem of "Why" is all about taking action. Abraham Lincoln said, "Things may come to those who wait, but only the things left by those who hustle." In truth, whatever we think or believe is of little consequence. The only consequence is what we do. That is essentially what James 2:14 says; *"What good is it, my brothers if someone says he has faith but does not have works? Can that faith save him?"*

One of my favorite stories of faith is one of a famous tightrope walker named Charles Blondin, who crossed Niagara Falls not once but numerous times on a one-inch-thick rope. This stunning feat made Mr. Blondin renowned starting in the summer of 1859. He walked 160 feet above the falls several times back and forth between Canada and the United States as huge crowds on both sides looked on with shock and awe. Once, Mr. Blondin crossed in a sack, once on stilts, another time on a bicycle, and once, he even carried a stove and cooked an omelet! He could have easily signed a "Red Bull" contract and made lots of money if he had only lived a century or two later. On July 15th, Blondin walked backward across the tightrope to Canada and returned pushing a wheelbarrow. One specific version of this story is told that it was after pushing a wheelbarrow across while blindfolded that Blondin asked for some audience participation. It is said that he asked his audience, "Do you believe I can carry a person across in this wheelbarrow?" Of course, the crowd shouted that yes, they believed! It was then that Blondin posed the question - "Who will get in the wheelbarrow?' Of course, no one did.

Some urban versions of the story say one man stepped forward from the audience and said I will do it. Maybe it was his agent sensing a chance to take this act to a whole new level. The man proceeded to get in the wheelbarrow, to the amazement of the crowd, and over the next 30 minutes, they both inched their way back across to the other side. If that part of the story is actual, then the man in the wheelbarrow would have been the only one who truly believed in Blondin that day!

The Solution

Talk is cheap. At some point, you must get in the wheelbarrow. Reject passivity, step up to the plate, get in the game, or jump in. However you choose to say it, you will need to exercise faith. It may be a step of faith or a real leap of faith, but that is when you discover the size of your "why." If your "why" is not big enough, you probably won't do it. When you take action, you engage your "Why," which triggers various secondary reactions. It lets you and those around you know that you are serious about your intention, and it gets their attention. Things that once seemed confusing become more apparent because your "why" becomes more evident. Things that seemed impossible suddenly became very possible.

For example, Admiral Robert Peary attempted to reach the North Pole seven times before finally achieving his goal. He had a big "why." Oscar Hammerstein produced five shows on Broadway that flopped before staging the smash hit Oklahoma, which more than 4.5 million people saw during a record-breaking run of 2,212 performances. He also had a big "why"! And don't forget Thomas Edison, who failed in his attempt to create a workable light bulb ten thousand times before creating one that finally worked. Can you imagine trying anything 10,000 times? I would say he had a big "why." Tenacity rewards those with lofty goals. It can also be noted that through tenacity, we earn the reward that comes with accomplishing our goals and having a strong "why" will keep you going when others stop. And that is why your "why" is vitally important!

No one exemplified that better than Jesus Christ, who had a purpose, goal, and mission greater than anyone else would attempt. To be the Savior of the world, redeeming mankind, and establishing His church to advance His kingdom throughout eternity is the ultimate mission. We know His "why" was to obey fully and please His Father God – *"To do the works of the Father and destroy the devil."* (**John 4:34; 1 John 3:8**). I also believe **Hebrews 12:2** gives us a picture of His "why" when it says, *"for the joy of accomplishing the goal set before Him, endured the cross."* Jesus modeled something I want in my life, and I would venture to say we all need at some point. That is an "action bias." There is rarely a perfect time to do anything. We can easily get stuck on "Ready, aim, aim, aim, but we never fire." Author and Pastor Mark Batterson says sometimes it's better just to say "Ready, Fire" and keep adjusting the aim as you move along. That means you may make a mistake or fail, but when you fail forward, you constantly learn to do it better. Why? Because that is the only way you will get to where you want to be.

The Truth

Sylvester Stallone was a struggling actor when he saw the boxing match between Chuck Wepner, a 30-1 underdog, and Muhammed Ali in a March 24, 1975 fight. This led him to write the original "Rocky" movie script, and it all came about because he had a "why," a belief that was big enough to overcome considerable odds in his own life. To go even further, the producers wanted someone else to play the main character, Rocky Balboa, but Stallone refused to sell the story unless he could play the main character. The prize for his "Big Why" was a film series that grossed over $1 Billion at the worldwide box office. That is a lot of earthly rewards for his step of faith. Read the following scriptures and consider how you might step out in faith, take a leap of faith, or take some action to see God do something new in your life that can have eternal rewards!

> *Proverbs 3:5-6 ESV Trust in the Lord with all your heart, and do not lean on your own understanding. In all your ways acknowledge him, and he will make straight your paths.*
>
> *2 Timothy 1:7 NLT For God has not given us a spirit of fear and timidity, but of power, love, and self-discipline.*
>
> *Deuteronomy 31:6 NLT So be strong and courageous! Do not be afraid and do not panic before them. For the*

Lord your God will personally go ahead of you. He will neither fail you nor abandon you."

1 Corinthians 16:13-14 NLT Be on guard. Stand firm in the faith. Be courageous. Be strong. And do everything with love.

II Corinthians 5:7 NKJV For we walk by faith, not by sight.

James 2:22 ESV You see that faith was active along with his works, and faith was completed by his works.

Romans 12:11 AMPC Never lag in zeal and in earnest endeavor; be aglow and burning with the Spirit, serving the Lord.

Before You Ever Had The Problem,
God Had The Solution.

NOTES

Week Four – Day Seven
Solutions From Five Faithful Friends
Reflect, Record, Rejoice

Reflect

Review the past 6 days of devotionals and reflect on what stood out from what you read. Did you get any new insight? Any new understanding of God's word? Did you discover any areas of your life that you need some solutions?

Record

Write down your thoughts from what you just reflected on, putting down any impressions you received on paper or in digital format. Ask God to give you insight into what He wants to show you from what He has spoken to you this past week.

Rejoice

Take time to express thanksgiving and joy to God for His Word and desire to speak to you, lead you, and give you solutions for living in faithful excellence. Make an intentional effort to find someone today with whom you can share what

Before You Ever Had The Problem, God Had The Solution.

you learned from your time with God this week in these readings and, most of all, through His Truth!

Week Five – Day One
Solutions For Dragon Slaying
They Faced Fear And Did It Anyway

The Problem

What would have happened to Abraham if he had allowed the fear of going to a land he had no fundamental knowledge of to keep him from going? What would have happened to Moses if he had let the fear of Pharaoh and the might of Egypt keep him from his mission from God? What about the fear Joshua, Esther, or Gideon felt? And what about Peter, Paul, and Mary (from the Bible, not the singing group), or the apostles and the early church? Most of all, what about Jesus, who sweat drops of blood as He prayed in the garden of Gethsemane before facing crucifixion on the cross? (**Matthew 26:36-42**). As you move forward, facing whatever challenge, obstacle, adversity, or opposition in life, you will have to confront your fears at some point. Sadly, most people let fear stop them from stepping out in faith and going after that dream of growing into the person they desire to be, and therein lies the problem for today.

The Solution

Do you really want to be like most people? Those listed above from the Bible were not unlike most of us as they faced real significant challenges, obstacles, and fears. However, though they felt the fear, they chose not to let it keep them from what they were called to or had to do. As the saying goes, "Feel the fear and do it anyway." In truth, most of the fears you and I will face in this life are not life-threatening, so I don't want to compare our situation too closely to those of these biblical heroes. However, we do have to be able to face whatever fear we encounter, identify it, and deal with it soundly. (**2 Timothy 1:7**). I think it is significant that God often said to these previously mentioned from the Bible narrative to *"Fear not," "Be strong and courageous," "Do not be dismayed," "Be confident and undaunted," "Do not be dismayed"* and other such phrases. (**Joshua 1:6-9; Isaiah 41:10; John 16:33**).

Almost any significant accomplishment in life requires taking a risk – do it anyway! I believe God has already provided a solution for every fear we may face in this life. In the practical growth steps of life, consider the first time you rode a bike, jumped off a high dive, decided to get married, or had your first child. These are all situations that may have produced paralyzing fear for you. Every time you face a fear and do it anyway, you build up more confidence to face the next one, bringing you closer to where you want to be. Whether it is just a step or a real leap of faith, overcoming that fear can transform your life. Even though it may be terrifying, embrace the fear with courageous faith and take action anyway. If you don't act, you may miss the opportunity to grow and become the person you want and are called to be.

The Truth

Take a few minutes to pray through the following verses and consider what God may be saying to you about facing your fears.

> *2 Timothy 1:7 NKJV "For God has not given us a spirit of fear, but of power and of love and of a sound mind."*

Joshua 1:6-7 NLT "Be strong and courageous, for you are the one who will lead these people to possess all the land I swore to their ancestors I would give them. 7 Be strong and very courageous. Be careful to obey all the instructions Moses gave you. Do not deviate from them, turning either to the right or to the left. Then you will be successful in everything you do.

Isaiah 41:10 AMPC "Fear not [there is nothing to fear], for I am with you; do not look around you in terror and be dismayed, for I am your God. I will strengthen and harden you to difficulties, yes, I will help you; yes, I will hold you up and retain you with My [victorious] right hand of rightness and justice."

John 16:33 AMPC "I have told you these things, so that in Me you may have [perfect] peace and confidence. In the world you have tribulation and trials and distress and frustration; but be of good cheer [take courage; be confident, certain, undaunted]! For I have overcome the world. [I have deprived it of power to harm you and have conquered it for you.]"

Before You Ever Had The Problem,
God Had The Solution.

NOTES

Week Five – Day Two
Solutions For Dragon Slaying
Draw Your Sword Of Boldness And Just Ask

The Problem

What if you actually could have had something you desperately wanted or needed but simply failed to ask for it? This is a very powerful but overlooked secret to solutions to many problems. It's also an essential spiritual principle of prayer. (**Luke 11:9-11**). So why do we fail to ask? Is it fear of looking needy, foolish, or stupid? Are you simply afraid of hearing the word "no," whether it's for something very small or a significant need? I know we talked about fear yesterday, but this failure to simply ask can also be fueled by fear and an obstacle to blessings coming your way. Consider that with this mindset of being afraid to ask, you essentially tell yourself "no" in advance. Maybe the problem is that nasty obstacle called pride. Yes, that human facade of not wanting to depend on anyone else. That is a legitimate problem as well, but it's another problem for another day. For now, let's look at some solutions for the "asking" issue.

The Solution

The foundational key to "asking" is this. Don't *assume* you will get a "no." You start by taking the risk to *"ask and keep on asking, seek and keep on seeking, knock and keep on knocking,"* as Jesus instructed in **Luke 11:9**. Even if the answer is "no," you're no worse off than you were when you started and if the answer is "yes" then you're a lot better off. What needs to be your mindset and attitude when you ask? <u>First</u>, *ask as if you expect to get it.* That is what **James 1:2-3** encourages. It is a spiritual principle of prayer, but it also applies to many other areas of life. With an expectation of faith, ask as if it has already been granted and hope for a "yes."

<u>Secondly</u>, *assume that it is possible to get what you are asking for,* with some exceptions. Yes, start with the assumption that you can get the upgrade, the table by the window, the contract you submitted the proposal for, or even that second date. Make sure those assumptions are at least somewhat realistic. For example, asking to pass a final exam after having not studied for it probably won't work. I know that one from experience!

<u>Thirdly</u>, *ask someone who can actually give it to you or do it for you.* An example would be the story in **Matthew 8:5-10** of the Roman officer who knew Jesus had the power to heal his servant. He was so confident that he simply asked Jesus to speak the word to heal his servant. Now, that is power <u>and</u> authority. Know <u>who</u> you need to speak to and ask them. <u>Fourth</u>, *be clear and specific.* In **James 1: 5** and **Luke 18:1-8** there are two great examples of the importance of being totally clear and very specific when we ask. Vague requests produce vague results every time!

Lastly, *Ask Repeatedly.* Again, the passage in **Luke 9:11-13** could be a seminar on how to ask. The key is persistence, and Jesus tells another story to illustrate this in **Luke 18:1-8**. Simply don't stop short, and don't give up! You must accept the fact there will be rejection along the way (we'll talk more about that tomorrow). Some days or even weeks, it may feel like lots of it. However, take heart because your mindset is to ask and keep asking, "For whoever asks and keeps on asking receives" (**Luke 11:13**). Children really understand this principle. Do you remember when you used to ask for stuff as a kid? There will be a "yes" sooner or later! We have encouragement from biblical heroes like Nehemiah and Esther, who made some big, risky, and dangerous requests. Look up their stories, be inspired, and remember, Just Ask!

The Truth

Take a few minutes to pray through the following verses and consider what God may be saying to you about taking your "ask" to a new level.

> *Luke 11:9-11 AMP "So I say to you, ask and keep on asking, and it will be given to you; seek and keep on seeking, and you will find; knock and keep on knocking, and the door will be opened to you. For everyone who keeps on asking [persistently], receives; and he who keeps on seeking [persistently], finds; and to him who keeps on knocking [persistently], the door will be opened."*

> *Matthew 8:5-10 NLT "When Jesus returned to Capernaum, a Roman officer came and pleaded with him, "Lord, my young servant lies in bed, paralyzed and in terrible pain." Jesus said, "I will come and heal him." But the officer said, "Lord, I am not worthy to have you come into my home. Just say the word from where you are, and my servant will be healed. I know this because I am under the authority of my superior officers, and I have authority over my soldiers. I only need to say,*

Before You Ever Had The Problem, God Had The Solution.

'Go,' and they go, or 'Come,' and they come. And if I say to my slaves, 'Do this,' they do it." When Jesus heard this, he was amazed. Turning to those who were following him, he said, "I tell you the truth, I haven't seen faith like this in all Israel!"

James 1:5 NLT "If you need wisdom, ask our generous God, and he will give it to you. He will not rebuke you for asking."

Week Five – Day Three
Solutions For Dragon Slaying
Rejection Is A Myth

The Problem

What if you never got rejected for anything, by anyone, anywhere. Accepted by everyone, in every school, organization, job, social club, you name it, you're in. The reality is that rejection is a natural part of life. If you don't believe that, you haven't experienced the world of dating and relationships. Rejection is not really the problem that I want to share today. The problem is this – "Rejection is a myth!" First, let me assure you that I have been rejected hundreds, if not thousands, of times in my life already. From not being picked for the all-star team to not getting the solo to not getting the scholarship, the job, the promotion, my song, or my book. Well, you get the idea. I understand the feeling and impact of rejection. But trust me, I'll be okay. One reason is that I have learned the powerful mind-shift that rejection is a myth. Amidst all this rejection, I have somehow survived, and I've still been abundantly, undeniably, and amazingly blessed. This idea that rejection is a myth really is a game-changer. So, if that is the problem, then what is the solution? I'm glad you asked!

The Solution

Did you know that rejection is simply a concept you have in your head? When you get a "no," the universal symbol for rejection, your situation doesn't get worse. It just stayed the same. It only gets worse when you take it personally and place your value on it. The truth is you don't have anything to lose by asking, and because there is something to possibly gain, why not ask? This is also a biblical principle from **Luke 11:9-13,** as seen in yesterday's reading.

This mindset slays the dragon of rejection whenever it raises its ugly head to cause you to experience fear of asking. It's also good to remember this "little" abbreviation, "SWSWSWSW." It stands for "some will, some won't, so what, someone's waiting" to say yes. Whenever you ask for anything from anyone, keep this in mind. Keep it in mind when you ask about simple things and eternal things, like sharing the good news of God's love and the gospel. This could change someone's eternity, so we can't let that old myth of rejection get in the way of such an important message. As **Romans 10:14-15** shows us, people will never get a chance to say "yes" to the gospel if they never hear the message of the gospel.

Winston Churchill had an interesting take on this concept. He said, "Success consists of going from failure to failure with no loss of enthusiasm." There are many incredible stories throughout the bible and the everyday lives of people who persevered through rejection to gain the prize. You will need to learn to reject rejection to get to the greatest prizes. When someone says no, you say, "Next!" One of the best examples of this mindset is the founder of Kentucky Fried Chicken (KFC). You have probably heard stories, seen commercials, or just caught a glimpse of the likeness of Colonel Harland Sanders with his unmistakable white hair, stylish beard, and three-piece suit. He left his home with his pressure cooker and a unique recipe for cooking Southern fried chicken, which, in my book, should be a staple in anyone's diet. He went on to receive 1,009 rejections before he found someone to believe in his dream. Now consider this: because he chose to believe rejection is a myth, there are over 18,900 KFC outlets in over 118 countries and territories worldwide!

I can't emphasize how important this L.I.F.E. Leadership Solution is for all areas of life but most of all for sharing the greatest message of the Gospel (**Luke 4:18-19**). If one person tells you no, ask someone else. Remember, there are over 8 billion people on the planet. Someone, somewhere, sometimes will say yes. Don't be paralyzed by the fear of rejection. Move on to that person who is waiting to say *YES!*

The Truth

Take a few minutes to pray through the following verses and consider what God may be saying to you about how you can begin to see rejection as a myth.

> *Romans 10:14-15 NKJV How then shall they call on Him in whom they have not believed? And how shall they believe in Him of whom they have not heard? And how shall they hear without a preacher? And how shall they preach unless they are sent? As it is written: "How beautiful are the feet of those who preach the gospel of peace, Who bring glad tidings of good things!"*

> *John 20:21 NKJV So Jesus said to them again, "Peace to you! As the Father has sent Me, I also send you."*

> *Luke 4:18-19 AMP "The Spirit of the Lord is upon Me (the Messiah), Because He has anointed Me to preach*

the good news to the poor. He has sent Me to announce release (pardon, forgiveness) to the captives, And recovery of sight to the blind, To set free those who are oppressed (downtrodden, bruised, crushed by tragedy), to proclaim the favorable year of the Lord [the day when salvation and the favor of God abound greatly]."

Week Five – Day Four
Solutions For Dragon Slaying
Be Willing To Pay The Price

The Problem

Sacrifice, pain, sweat, discipline. These are all words that most people don't want to hear. On the other hand, behind any worthwhile goal or accomplishment, there is usually a story of training, practice, discipline, and sacrifice. It could be the price of pursuing one thing with a singular focus while putting everything else in your life on hold. It could be the price of investing your own personal resources, time, and energy for that one opportunity to see that BHAG (Big Hairy Audacious Goal) accomplished. Whatever it is, the willingness to do what's required and, more often, above and beyond what is required adds that extra dimension needed to persevere in the face of overwhelming challenges, setbacks, and sacrifice. You have to take on the mindset that the pain is only temporary and the prize is worth it all.

As I type these words, the world is preparing for the 2024 Summer Olympics in Paris, France, where over 11,000 athletes from around the globe will exhibit this type of willingness to pay the price. One of the most remarkable stories of this was from the 1976 games when a Japanese gymnast named Shun Fujimoto landed a perfect triple-somersault twist dismount from the rings – on a *broken right knee!* It was a remarkable display of courage, determination, and maybe insanity. In the interview afterward, he remarked,

Before You Ever Had The Problem, God Had The Solution.

"The pain shot through me like a knife, bringing tears to my eyes. But now I have the gold medal, and the pain is nothing." What gave this young man extraordinary courage in the face of excruciating pain and the severe risk of a long-term injury? Simply put, it was the prize! You are on your way to the solution when you understand the prize.

The Solution

All great athletes, musicians, salespeople, and best of the best, all-pro, first chair in whatever field knows that it takes practice, determination, and doing it better consistently to excel in that field. After a concert, a middle-aged woman once confronted Legendary Violinist Issac Stern, saying, "Oh, I would give my life to being able to play like you!" To which Stern replied, "Lady, that I did!" It's a commitment to pursue a specific goal that helps anyone do remarkable things. When it comes to what matters most, Jesus had some things to say about being willing to pay the price. In **Luke 14:28-30** He says to count the cost before you step out. Jesus makes it clear that we are to sit down and count the cost before saying we want something. You may discover that some of the costs are more than you are willing to pay. You must weigh all the factors. It's a critical Life Leadership Solution because it establishes the resolve and determination to press on and fight through when it gets hard once you determine that the prize is worth it.

The Truth

Take a few minutes to pray through the following verses and consider what God may be saying to you about being willing to pay the price;

Luke 14:28-30 ESV For which of you, desiring to build a tower, does not first sit down and count the cost, whether he has enough to complete it? 29 Otherwise, when he has laid a foundation and is not able to finish, all who see it begin to mock him, 30 saying, 'This man began to build and was not able to finish.'

2 Timothy 2:3-4 AMP Take with me your share of hardship [passing through the difficulties which you are called to endure], like a good soldier of Christ Jesus. No soldier in active service gets entangled in the [ordinary business] affairs of civilian life; [he avoids them] so that he may please the one who enlisted him to serve.

Hebrews 12:11 ESV For the moment all discipline seems painful rather than pleasant, but later it yields the peaceful fruit of righteousness to those who have been trained by it.

Before You Ever Had The Problem,
God Had The Solution.

NOTES

Week Five – Day Five
Solutions For Dragon Slaying
God Said I Could, So I Did

The Problem

One of the biggest problems you will face regularly is the temptation to drive through life with the psychological brakes on. Many people do this by staying in a comfort zone of their own making, maintaining inaccurate beliefs about life, or getting stuck in self-doubt. That is a problem if it is your story, but I'm happy to tell you there is good news because there is a solution. The truth is this: almost everything you want is just outside your comfort zone. What will it take for you to release the brakes of your fears and replace your limiting false beliefs with Truth? How do you change your mindset to faith and confidence in what God says? The comfort zone is a prison constructed by the enemy of your soul, and his plans for you are never good. They are filled with a collection of "you can't," "you'll never," and countless other negative thoughts accumulated and reinforced by other lies you have been told throughout your life. Do you see how this could be a real problem? Are you living it now? Well, again, I've got good news! If God says you can, will you?

The Solution

Rather than training to *limit* yourself, consider training yourself to *release* yourself to believe. It's like the classic illustration of the baby elephant in the circus

135

tied to a stake with a rope when the trainers teach it to stay. At this stage in the elephant's growth, the rope can still keep the baby elephant from getting away. However, over time, the same stake and rope can hold the same creature once it becomes a mature 5-ton adult elephant simply because the elephant has been programmed to think the same rope is still strong enough. Don't be an elephant!

You have the power and freedom to choose to stop re-creating the same negative, fear-filled, limiting thoughts over and over. You can change the bad reruns playing, the stifling stories you are telling yourself, and any beliefs that are holding you back. It is the biblical principle of renewing your mind (**Romans 12:1-2**), changing your mindset (**Colossians 3:1-2**), and thinking better thoughts (**Philippians 4:8**).

As long as we settle for complaining about our present circumstances and what we don't have, our mind will stay focused on that rather than the higher, better thoughts. What if you set your mind on what you are grateful for, expressed gratitude in as many ways as possible, and released the brakes on your joy? Your level of gratitude is dynamically attached to the level of joy you will experience in this life. We get to choose the cycle we want to experience. One that cycles our thought life up to higher thoughts or one that drags us down to the junky stuff. If we want the higher stuff, we must flood our minds with truth from God's word and thoughts centered on a Kingdom of God mindset of righteousness, peace, and joy. (**Romans 14:17**). As Albert Einstein once said, "The significant problems we face cannot be solved by the same level of thinking that creates them." Higher thoughts for higher solutions!

One of the simple solutions for this that I have practiced over the years is scriptural affirmations and confessions. Peter Lord, who authored several books, including "Hearing God," "Soul Care," and "Bless and Be Blessed," taught me this practice years ago when I had the privilege of serving with him at Park Avenue Baptist Church in Titusville, Florida. These are based on various scriptures and simply affirm God's truth declared over our lives. I have included a few of these in the appendix at the back of the book, and I urge you to try some of these in your own life. You can even create your own personal scripture affirmations, which I strongly encourage you to do. Just read or speak them out loud over your life and choose to believe them. Here are a few other guidelines for creating your own affirmations and confessions from scripture:

1. Start with the words "*I am.*"
These are two of the most powerful words in the English language. Always be aware of whatever words you choose to connect with the words "I am." You are declaring this over yourself and reinforcing it in your life every time you speak it.

2. Make it scriptural and specific
Vague affirmations produce vague results.

3. Review them, read them, and repeat them daily
You are creating a new mindset and a new way of thinking.

The Truth

Before You Ever Had The Problem, God Had The Solution.

Take a few minutes to pray through the following verses and consider creating your own scriptural affirmations or confessions based on one of the verses;

> *Romans 12:1-2 NLT And so, dear brothers and sisters, I plead with you to give your bodies to God because of all he has done for you. Let them be a living and holy sacrifice—the kind he will find acceptable. This is truly the way to worship him. Don't copy the behavior and customs of this world, but let God transform you into a new person by changing the way you think. Then you will learn to know God's will for you, which is good and pleasing and perfect.*

> *Colossians 3:1-2 NKJV If then you were raised with Christ, seek those things which are above, where Christ is, sitting at the right hand of God. Set your mind on things above, not on things on the earth.*

> *Philippians 4:8 AMP Finally, believers, whatever is true, whatever is honorable and worthy of respect, whatever is right and confirmed by God's word, whatever is pure and wholesome, whatever is lovely and brings peace, whatever is admirable and of good repute; if there is any excellence, if there is anything worthy of praise, think continually on these things [center your mind on them, and implant them in your heart].*

Week Five – Day Six
Solutions For Dragon Slaying
Keep Your Eyes On The Prize

The Problem

What happens when you have your eyes on the wrong prize? Or what if you wake up one day and realize that the ladder of success you have been climbing is leaning against the wrong building? It reminds me of some very practical advice that says, "You don't need a parachute to skydive; you only need a parachute to skydive twice." (I wouldn't encourage you to test that in real life, by the way). Back to the prize. When you fail to keep your eyes on the prize, you can easily get discouraged and want to give up.

The process is not always fun, but it is part of the commitment required to obtain the prize. **1 Corinthians 9:24** speaks of "running the race in such a way to win." It takes focus and determination to avoid distractions, which can be a major problem that keeps you from running a good race. (**Galatians 5:7**). When you realize you are off course, it's an even bigger problem if you don't face the reality that you are headed in the wrong direction.

The first step is to get out of the river, which is called "de-nile" (denial). If the fruit you see is not your desired fruit, it's time to change the seeds you've been planting (**Galatians 6:7-9**). Doing more of what isn't working will not make it any better. It's like the husband who refused to ask for directions or even use a GPS while on a trip with his wife, all the while knowing he was getting increasingly lost. Finally, after his wife convinced him they were way off course, he replied, "Well honey, we may be lost, but we're making great time."

Now, that's a problem that needs some immediate attention. Facts do not cease to exist because we ignore them. Only when we dare to face the music, heed the warning signs, and take appropriate action, no matter how uncomfortable it may be, will we see the change we desire.

The Solution

Are there yellow lights going off on your life dashboard? It's wise to take action concerning the yellow lights before they turn red. To ignore these warning signs is to risk something much worse. Much like the guy who put a piece of black tape over the check engine light in his car, thinking the problem will just go away if he can't see it. The better solution is to deal with the flashing lights, and in our case, it is to make an intentional decision not to tolerate anything that keeps you from running a race that matters.

God is often doing a work in our lives, even when we can't see clearly what He is doing (**Philippians 1:6**). The key is to look to God for the strength to cooperate with this work He is doing in your life, not in your strength as stated in **Philippians 2:13**. In reality, the problem is usually less painful to resolve and more manageable to solve when we humbly admit that we got off track. That is when we can return to the race and obtain the prize. It's like an alcoholic or even a workaholic who loses his marriage, family, or health before he realizes what it is costing him. The excuses start sounding so good that he even begins to believe them. Often, the failure to face what isn't working is fear. It doesn't always have to be a drastic solution, but it does require you to act, so why not do it now? Why wait? What's holding you back? Here are a few possible action steps:

1. **Take a few minutes to make a list of areas in your life that you would like to see changed or improved.**

2. **Don't make it a gripe or complain session but a dream session of what could be.**

3. **Who can you ask to help you? Do you need to ask an expert, coach, or mentor to guide you to the desired improvement or change?**

4. **Make a plan, take one step at a time, and ask God to give you the courage to persevere to the prize!**

The Truth

Take a few minutes to pray through the following verses and consider how God's word can encourage you to run your race in a way that will help you to win.

> *1 Corinthians 9:24 AMP Do you not know that in a race all the runners run [their very best to win], but only one receives the prize? Run [your race] in such a way that you may seize the prize and make it yours!*

> *Galatians 5:7 NIV You were running a good race. Who cut in on you to keep you from obeying the truth?*

Before You Ever Had The Problem, God Had The Solution.

Galatians 6:7-9 ESV Do not be deceived: God is not mocked, for whatever one sows, that will he also reap. 8 For the one who sows to his own flesh will from the flesh reap corruption, but the one who sows to the Spirit will from the Spirit reap eternal life. 9 And let us not grow weary of doing good, for in due season we will reap, if we do not give up.

Philippians 1:6 AMP I am convinced and confident of this very thing, that He who has begun a good work in you will [continue to] perfect and complete it until the day of Christ Jesus [the time of His return].

Philippians 2:13 AMP For it is [not your strength, but it is] God who is effectively at work in you, both to will and to work [that is, strengthening, energizing, and creating in you the longing and the ability to fulfill your purpose] for His good pleasure.

Week Five – Day Seven
Solutions For Dragon Slaying
Reflect, Record, Rejoice

Reflect

Review the past 6 days of devotionals and reflect on what stood out from what you read. Did you get any new insight? Any new understanding of God's word? Did you discover any areas of your life that you need some solutions?

Record

Write down your thoughts from what you just reflected on, putting down any impressions you received on paper or in digital format. Ask God to give you insight into what He wants to show you from what He has spoken to you this past week.

Rejoice

Take time to express thanksgiving and joy to God for His Word, for His desire to speak to you, lead you, and give you solutions for living in faithful excellence.

Before You Ever Had The Problem,
God Had The Solution.

Make an intentional effort to find someone today with whom you can share what you learned from your time with God this week in these readings, your prayer time, and most of all, through His Word!

Week Six – Day One
Essentials For Living In Faithful Excellence
The One Thing I Must Do

The Problem

When you wake up tomorrow morning, what will be the most important thing on your agenda that day? A looming deadline, an exam, an event you've been looking forward to for some time, or something you've been avoiding. We all have some sort of agenda each day, and if we don't have one of our own, someone else may have one for us. Now, that can be a big problem.

I have a little quote someone gave me years ago that I keep handy: "The most important thing on my agenda today is to let be, be still, and know that He is God." For me, that is helpful because it reminds me that **1)** I *will* follow an agenda that day – mine or someone else's, and **2)** the *most important* thing is *"Be still and know,"* by experience, by understanding, by an encounter that **3)** *"He is God"* and I'm not. That helps me to keep things in perspective.

This idea of "the one thing I must do" forces us to narrow our focus. It requires us to cut away the extras and get to the essentials. For example, when a person is drowning, the "one thing" is air. When thirsty, the "one thing" is water, and when hungry, the "one thing" is food. You will find that they are entirely intentional, deliberate, and focused on finding that "one thing."

Before You Ever Had The Problem,
God Had The Solution.

Have you ever been around someone who was "*hangry?*" What is "HANGRY?" It's that nasty combination of hunger for food and anger at not getting it yet. Everything else is secondary to that pursuit of eating. It is a relentless, desperate act and a good picture of a hungry heart that seeks God, as David was talking about in **Psalms 27:4**. He had made a valuable discovery by this point in his life that God's presence was simply not an option. It was his refuge, his shelter, his high tower, his shield, his rampart, his stronghold, and his secret place. As Rick Warren, author and former Senior Pastor of Saddleback Church, says, "The closer you live to God, the smaller everything else appears."

In the New Testament, Mary gives us a picture of a heart and life seeking "one thing." Jesus was so impressed and captured by her determination that He commended her publicly for it. **(Luke 10:38-42).** In verse 42, He says, *"Mary has discovered it and it won't be taken away from her."* Have you discovered it? This pearl of great price, this treasure like no other, this "one thing" more remarkable than anything else? Mary could have been doing a lot of different practical and worthwhile things. So, what caused her to sit at the feet of Jesus rather than serve His hand? Serving His hand would have been a good choice but not the best option.

This is a challenge set before us daily. With the overload of life's pressures before us and the "urgent stack" climbing higher by the minute, it seems more challenging each day to stop and sit in the presence of Jesus and listen to His voice. Why does the pressure of even "good things" seem to squeeze out the best? It is costly to choose "one thing" above everything else. The apostle Paul talks about the one thing in **Philippians 3:13-14** by saying, *"...but one thing I do; forgetting what lies behind and straining forward to what lies ahead, I press on toward the goal to win the prize...."* That prize is Jesus, His presence, and His Kingdom in our lives. To choose to forget what lies behind and to press on is not an easy task and sometimes possibly one of our greatest challenges.

The Solution

It takes determination, persistence, and commitment to pursue one thing above all others. As Soren Kierkegaard once wrote, "You only have time for one passion in life. Choose your passion carefully." Jesus Christ is the only prize worthy of our greatest passion and pursuit. As the saying goes, one committed person will accomplish more than a thousand people with interest alone.

An amazing story of persistence and survival is that of Tsutomu Yamaguchi. At the close of World War II, he amazingly survived the atomic bombing of Hiroshima, Japan. Following the bombing, he was taken to a hospital in Nagasaki, where he then survived another atomic bombing. He went on to recover and live a productive life until he passed away on January 4th, 2011, at the age of 93. This guy survived two nuclear disasters, made a comeback, and lived a long, productive life. Simply remarkable!

The first vital solution for living in faithful excellence is understanding this "one thing" you must do. As **Psalm 27:4** says, *"One thing I have asked of the Lord, that will I seek...."* Other versions say, *"One thing I have asked of the Lord, this only do I seek..."* or *"One thing I have asked of the Lord, that I will seek, inquire for and insistently require...."* Whatever version you read, it comes down to "one thing." If you could ask God for one thing, what would it be? How valuable or priceless is being in His presence and gaining His Kingdom life?

Jesus commands us in **Matthew 6:33** to *"But seek first the Kingdom of God and His righteousness, and all of these things will be added to you."* This is a very clear instruction from Jesus, and it clearly brings it all down to one thing.

Countless people are spending their lives looking for something to fill the void that was created by God Himself for His presence. They are searching hard for anything to fill the emptiness and the emptiness that gnaws at them daily. Maybe a relationship will do it. Perhaps a certain degree of fame, material gain, or personal achievement is what they are seeking to fill the void. Maybe all of those have failed, and now they are seeking a drug or alcohol high or lifestyle of pleasure that will deal with the craving that yearns for this emptiness to be satisfied.

Even some who profess to know God often find themselves seeking the wrong things to fill that place that belongs only to God. Religious activity, family life, and even ministry ambition can all be lesser substitutes for the "one thing." Where is your treasure? Where is your heart? What are you seeking above all else? Is it worth the price you are paying to gain it? *"What if a person gains the whole world and yet loses his soul?"* as Jesus asked in **Matthew 16:26**. These are critical life leadership questions, and each of us will answer them today by what and whom we choose to seek.

The Truth

Take a few minutes to pray through the following verses and consider how God's word can give you encouragement to choose the greatest treasure and make your time with him the one thing you must do;

Psalms 27:4 NIV One thing I ask from the Lord , this only do I seek: that I may dwell in the house of the Lord all the days of my life, to gaze on the beauty of the Lord and to seek him in his temple.

Matthew 6:33 AMP But first and most importantly seek (aim at, strive after) His kingdom and His righteousness [His way of doing and being right—the attitude and character of God], and all these things will be given to you also.

Matthew 16:25-26 ESV For whoever would save his life will lose it, but whoever loses his life for my sake will find it. 26 For what will it profit a man if he gains the whole world and forfeits his soul? Or what shall a man give in return for his soul?

Matthew 13:44-46 NKJV Again, the kingdom of heaven is like treasure hidden in a field, which a man found and hid; and for joy over it he goes and sells all that he has and buys that field. Again, the kingdom of heaven is like a merchant seeking beautiful pearls, who, when he had found one pearl of great price, went and sold all that he had and bought it.

Philippians 3:13-14 AMP Brothers and sisters, I do not consider that I have made it my own yet; but one thing I do: forgetting what lies behind and reaching forward to what lies ahead, I press on toward the goal to win

Before You Ever Had The Problem, God Had The Solution.

the [heavenly] prize of the upward call of God in Christ Jesus.

Week Six – Day Two
Essentials For Living In Faithful Excellence
Where You Dwell, You Swell

The Problem

Where do you choose to dwell? We have incredible freedom and personal power to decide where we want to dwell. Do you dwell on the positive or the negative? Or maybe you consider yourself a realist, so you would say you dwell in reality. Do you dwell on the problems or the possibilities? As Charlie Brown said, "I've developed a new philosophy: I only dread one day at a time." That is a rather bleak place to dwell.

In 1934, Charles B. Darrow of Germantown, Pennsylvania, was unemployed. He could have spent his days dwelling on his predicament or the bad break he was experiencing but instead chose to dwell on something more enjoyable. To amuse himself and pass the time, he created a board game that provided a possibility for supporting his family. That game is called "Monopoly," which became one of the best, if not the best-selling, board games in the world. Today it's sold in 80 countries, produced in 26 languages, and has such spin-offs as "Mayberry-opoly"(for fans of the Andy Griffith Show) and "Dawg-opoly"(for fans of the University of Georgia football). I happen to possess both of those spin-offs, as well as the original version, so I am a fan of the game. I would say Mr. Darrow's choice of *dwelling* and the *swelling* that followed paid off very well.

Before You Ever Had The Problem, God Had The Solution.

Dwell is one of the words King David used when he described *"the one thing he desired the most."* Dwelling is what you do when you remain on the same thing or in the same place. However, David was very specific about where he wanted to dwell. For him, it was *"the house of the Lord"* **(Psalm 27:4)**. David meant the very presence of God, not an actual building. Where you dwell matters. If you will, consider the "law of life," meaning we all become what we behold. At any given moment, you and I can choose to pay attention to what's present or missing, what's working or broken, what you have achieved, or where you've really blown it. This "where you dwell, you swell" idea can be good or bad news, depending on where you choose to dwell. That is the problem we will look at today, and I believe we will find some great solutions.

The Solution

Right now, your thoughts are leading you in a specific direction. One of the most important ways to lead your life is to lead your thoughts. This is how we choose to dwell and in what ways we eventually swell. In choosing where to dwell, you also win or lose the battle for your mind, thinking either overcoming thoughts or thoughts of defeat. Whatever you choose to dwell upon becomes increasingly conscious in your mind. This is also known as the cognitive principle of attention. In other words, focus creates feeling. I believe this is where we discover the joy of where we dwell. The more I dwell on thoughts of joy, the more joy I feel. The more I dwell on what I am thankful for, the more I am grateful. Conversely, the more you dwell on your worries, anxieties, and fears, the more you can be sure you will get them. I don't know about you, but I know what I want more of in my life.

This solution works for your spiritual life, relationships, work, and health. I would encourage you to try it in every area of life. I'm not talking about "think happy thoughts" pop psychology. I'm referring to a Biblical principle found throughout scripture that I consider one of the most essential solutions for "Living in Faithful Excellence." You'll find it in **Proverbs 23:7, Romans 12:1-2, Philippians 4:8, Colossians 3:1-17,** and several other places in the Bible. There are also incredible promises from Jesus concerning dwelling or abiding in Him. **John 15:7** says, *"If you abide in me and my words abide in you, you will ask what you desire, and it shall be done for you."* That is a fantastic promise, and it is fulfilled simply out of that abiding relationship with Jesus. Again, there is no better place to dwell and swell!

An image that I would like you to consider for this dwelling or abiding practice is that of a *sponge*. When dwelling in God's presence, I see myself as a sponge, soaking in Him. A sponge will always soak up whatever liquid that it is placed in. So, if I soak it in water, it won't squeeze out orange juice. I can choose to dwell continually or soak myself in God's presence and, like a sponge, be filled with Him so that when life squeezes me, He comes out. As I am immersed in His "living water," I can swell up with His life, and then that life flows out of me. The secret is to be intentional and relentless about *where* you choose to dwell. I encourage you to dwell with Christ today, soaking in His presence where you drip with His love, grace, and mercy throughout everyone you encounter. And keep returning for more because this source of living water, His river of life, never runs dry! (**Psalm 36:7-9**).

The Truth

Take a few minutes to pray through the following verses and consider how God's word can encourage you to choose to dwell in Him;

Psalms 27:4 NIV One thing I ask from the Lord , this only do I seek: that I may dwell in the house of the Lord all the days of my life, to gaze on the beauty of the Lord and to seek him in his temple.

Proverbs 23:7 NKJV For as he thinks in his heart, so is he. "Eat and drink!" he says to you, But his heart is not with you.

John 15:7 AMPC If you live in Me [abide vitally united to Me] and My words remain in you and continue to live in your hearts, ask whatever you will, and it shall be done for you.

Philippians 4:8 AMPC For the rest, brethren, whatever is true, whatever is worthy of reverence and is honorable and seemly, whatever is just, whatever is pure, whatever is lovely and lovable, whatever is kind and winsome and gracious, if there is any virtue and excellence, if there is anything worthy of praise, think on and weigh and take account of these things [fix your minds on them].

Colossians 3:1-2 AMPC IF THEN you have been raised with Christ [to a new life, thus sharing His resurrection from the dead], aim at and seek the [rich, eternal treasures] that are above, where Christ is, seated at the right hand of God. And set your minds and keep them set on what is above (the higher things), not on the things that are on the earth.

Before You Ever Had The Problem,
God Had The Solution.

NOTES

Week Six– Day Three
Essentials For Living In Faithful Excellence
We Always Conquer By Love

The Problem

Without a doubt, love was the foundational motivating force for Jesus' mission on earth. He was sent here in the first place because of love, as we read from **John 3:16**, *"For God so loved the world that He gave His only son into the world that through Him we might be saved."* Many have heard that verse so often that we sometimes allow it to become too familiar and minimize its significance. The singular focus of Jesus in redeeming us was driven by His love for the Father, His love for others, and His passionate pursuit of obeying the Father's purposes, even to the point of death on the cross. Just as Jesus conquered sin and death through His ultimate act of love, we, too, will always conquer by His love. **John 15:13** tells us there is no greater love than this love.

The problem is that we don't have the ability in ourselves to love this way. It's possible to come close to loving our spouse, family, or close friends with self-sacrificial love, even to the point that we would give our lives for them. But what would it take to love someone in this way who hates us, hurts us, or rejects us? Maybe you feel like the little girl who prayed, "Dear God, I bet it's hard for you to love everyone in the whole world. There are only four people in our family, and I don't even have enough for them." In describing the

157

sacrificial love of Jesus, **Romans 5:8** says, *"God demonstrated His love for us in this way, while we were his enemies Christ died for us."* That is the conquering love I am talking about here, so how do we receive this amazing love and express the conquering power of this love to others? Let's look at one solution from God's word.

The Solution

It takes a deliberate decision even to attempt to love like Christ but also requires honesty and humility to admit we don't have the power to do it ourselves. As **2 Corinthians 5:14** says, *"The love of Christ compels us..."* or as one version says, *"Christ's love has moved me to such extremes. His love is the first and last word in everything we do."* That is the power of this love when compelled by Christ in us and through us. The essential key to living out this love is best described in **Philippians 2:13,** which says, *"Not in your own strength for it is God Who is all the while effectually at work in you, energizing and creating in you the power and the desire, both to will and to work for His good pleasure and satisfaction and delight."* So, it is both surrendering to God's power working in us and working it out to make the intentional decision and effort to practically love with His love. To conquer by love in this way requires at least these three things of us.

1. *Be Deliberate*

Being deliberate in conquering by love is not done by accident, in that Christ's love compels us to be proactive by actual words and deeds.

2. *Be Consistent*

Be consistent to conquer. If we are to conquer by love, we must remember that it is a journey, not an event or project. It requires daily, weekly, and yearly follow-through.

3. *Be <u>Willful</u>*

Being willful to conquer by love is a choice of the will, and that is why we need God's powerful love working in us, energizing and creating in us the desire to both will and do his good pleasure of being vessels of His love.

There is a big difference between good intentions and intentional living. Simply cultivating good intentions without purposeful action can lead to frustration and unfulfillment. This is especially true in how we love. When Christians learn to conquer by love through our words, actions, and reactions, we will see a radical response from those who have never experienced this love. It has been said that on that final day, we will not be asked how much we did for God's kingdom, how much we gave to God's kingdom, or how many knew our name in God's kingdom but rather simply how we loved. Jesus told us clearly in **John 13:35,** *"By this all will know that you are my disciples, if you have love for one another."*

So, what does it look like to practically walk out this conquering love in our daily lives? The apostle Paul gives us a great picture in 1 Corinthians 13:4-8. Often referred to as "The Love Chapter," a modern-day translation of these verses puts it this way:

- **Love is large and incredibly patient**
- **Love is gentle and consistently kind to all**
- **Love refuses to be jealous when a blessing comes to someone else**

- **Love does not brag about one's own achievement nor inflate its own importance**
- **Love does not traffic in shame or disrespect nor selfishly seek its own honor**
- **Love is not easily irritated or quick to take offense**
- **Love joyfully celebrates honesty and finds no delight in what is wrong**
- **Love is a place of safety, for it never stops believing in the best for others**
- **Love never takes failure as defeat, for it never gives up**

Or, as I like to say, "We Always Conquer by Love!" In 1970, David and Barbara Green took out a $600 loan to make miniature picture frames from their home. Two years later, the fledgling enterprise opened a 300-square-foot store in Oklahoma City, and Hobby Lobby was born. Today, with more than 1,000 stores, Hobby Lobby is the world's largest privately owned arts and crafts retailer, with over 46,000 employees operating in 48 states. One of their stated core values is "Honoring the Lord in all we do by operating in a manner consistent with Biblical principles." That is a great foundation to build on, and it seems to have worked for them. You may or may not be a Hobby Lobby fan, but sometimes, I think it's just good to go to Hobby Lobby to read the inspirational quotes on some of the items they have for sale. One of my favorite ones I read on a recent visit was encouragement for practicing love in marriage relationships. "Marriage Rules: The first to apologize is *the bravest,* the first to forgive is *the strongest,* and the first to forget is *the happiest!*" Now, that is an excellent way to conquer by love!

The Truth

Take a few minutes to pray through the following verses and consider how God's word encourages and strengthens you to "Always Conquer by Love";

John 15:13 NKJV Greater love has no one than this, than to lay down one's life for his friends.

Romans 5:8 AMP But God clearly shows and proves His own love for us, by the fact that while we were still sinners, Christ died for us.

Philippians 2:13 AMPC [Not in your own strength] for it is God Who is all the while effectually at work in you [energizing and creating in you the power and desire], both to will and to work for His good pleasure and satisfaction and delight.

2 Corinthians 5:14 AMP For the love of Christ controls and compels us, because we have concluded this, that One died for all, therefore all died;

John 13:35 AMP By this everyone will know that you are My disciples, if you have love and unselfish concern for one another."

1 Corinthians 13:4-8 NIV Love is patient, love is kind. It does not envy, it does not boast, it is not proud. 5 It does not dishonor others, it is not self-seeking, it is not easily angered, it keeps no record of wrongs. 6 Love does not delight in evil but rejoices with the truth. 7 It always protects, always trusts, always hopes, always perseveres. 8 Love never fails.

Before You Ever Had The Problem,
God Had The Solution.

NOTES

Week Six – Day Four
Essentials For Living In Faithful Excellence
Practice Chronic Thankfulness

The Problem

I want to take a few minutes today to share a condition that plagues our society on every level. It is a problem for the young and old, rich and poor, regardless of gender or origin. It's commonly known as GDS, or "Gratitude Deficiency Syndrome." Do you or someone you know suffer from GDS, even mild to moderate GDS (okay, this is starting to sound like one of those pharmaceutical commercials)? Seriously though, this problem is real, and discovering the solution has been one of my life's most valuable, joy-producing benefits. Gratitude is a conviction, a practice, and a discipline. It can't be bought in a store or purchased online. The real irony is that you may see just the opposite if you go shopping on "Black Friday" or "Blue Saturday," the two largest shopping days of the year, which immediately follow "Thanksgiving Day" (did I mention how ironic that is?). On the other hand, a simple attitude of gratitude can change the atmosphere in a room and the direction of a conversation, and it can even affect the trajectory of your life.

So, what are some of the symptoms of "Gratitude Deficiency Syndrome" (GDS)? First, those with GDS are often disconnected from God on some level. **Psalm 100:4** tells us that thanksgiving or gratitude is the way we enter God's presence. Inversely, GDS sufferers could be unintentionally shutting themselves out of God's presence by not being grateful. Another symptom of GDS is being overindulgent in BNN. That is the "Bad News Network," which is the basic content of most social media, culture commentary, news outlets, and the negative bombardment of information that hits us daily. A third symptom that is seen often in GDS is a feeling of entitlement. Nothing will crush gratitude, contentment, and joy in your life as quickly as an attitude of entitlement. With this mindset, even when we receive something, we see it as a right, not a gift.

A fourth symptom that is often seen with GDS is the tendency to feed on worry and fear. It results from dwelling on what you hope won't happen, but fear probably will. And as we learned on day two of this week, "Where you dwell, you swell." Worry and fear want us to trust them more than we trust God, which is never a good idea. When discussing the solution, we will look at an excellent prescription for this in **Philippians 4:6-7**. The last symptom I want to mention is that GDS is usually a sign of CDS (Continuous Deficiency Syndrome). With CDS, you are always aware and frustrated that you could or should have more. Pastor and Author Andy Stanley calls this "Living in the land of Er." You always focus on how you could, should, or would be rich-er, smart-er, pretty-er, or whatever-er, if only. The consumer society we live in fuels this discontentment by constantly telling us in numerous ways that we need more and can't be content without more. Well, are you suffering from GDS? Most of us do on some level at some time in our lives. The good news is that there is a solution, and that is what this book is all about.

The Solution

It starts by focusing on your thoughts, words and attention to what is present and working rather than what is absent and deficient. You have the power and responsibility to shine the spotlight wherever you choose. Let's ask this vital question to begin with. "Why should you practice chronic thankfulness?" Remember, the *how* and the *what* won't matter if your *why* is not big enough. First and foremost, you experience more joy, which is a HUGE "why" for me.

As you have discovered, I like to keep it simple, so let's start with something we take for granted all the time – water. When were you last thankful for a sip of clean water? Or what about a bottle of cold water on a hot day? How about the way you can just turn on a faucet and get as much water as you want? Water has no caloric value, yet it's vital to our survival. It's overlooked and underappreciated by most of us most of the time. But if we learned to recognize and appreciate something as simple as water, we might crack the joy code. Mark Batterson, author and Senior Pastor of National Community Church, puts it this way; "Joy is not getting what you want. It's fully appreciating what you have, and it starts with the basics, like water and a million other moment-by-moment miracles."

A second byproduct of practicing Chronic Thankfulness is that you'll be more pleasant to be around. Gratitude is like a magnetic force that draws people just as an ingrate is someone no one enjoys being around. Let me see your hand. I know you have been there. You're having a pretty good day, and then you get around a whining, complaining, ungrateful person, and it just sucks the life and joy right out of your day. Not attractive or desirable. The third and the most important reason, as far as I am concerned, is that it's God's will for us, according to **1 Thessalonians 5:16-18**. *"Rejoice always, pray continually, give thanks in all circumstances; for this is God's will for you in Christ Jesus."* Giving thanks in all circumstances is how we do a gratitude mental gear shift. When we raise our view of our life, we raise how we experience our life. Practically speaking, it's choosing not to focus on that annoying habit of our spouse and instead focusing on how grateful we are that they overlook our annoying habits! That is a full-time job for my wife, and I am very grateful to her for that. Here are three basic things to remember and practice for Chronic Thankfulness from best-selling author and Life Coach Tommy Newberry.

1. Gratitude is a <u>Choice</u>

It comes from the will, and we all have the incredible power of choice. How will you use yours?

2. Gratitude is a <u>Feeling</u>

When we feel grateful, it does not mean our life is always great or we never have any challenges or issues. It just means that we focus our thoughts, words, and feelings on the blessings around us. Focus fuels feeling, and gratitude fuels joy!

3. Gratitude is a <u>Capacity</u>

This is great news because it means we can grow in our gratitude. We are not born with an attitude of gratitude or, for that matter, a mindset of entitlement. Either one is developed or increased by where we choose to dwell.

The Truth

Take a few minutes to answer the following questions and pray through the following verses to consider how they might encourage you to practice chronic thankfulness and pursue gratitude relentlessly. You don't have to wait until Thanksgiving to grow in your gratitude capacity.

> *Psalms 100:4 NASB Enter His gates with thanksgiving And His courts with praise. Give thanks to Him, bless His name.*

> *Philippians 4:6-7 NIV Do not be anxious about anything, but in every situation, by prayer and petition, with thanksgiving, present your requests to God. And the peace of God, which transcends all understanding, will guard your hearts and your minds in Christ Jesus.*

> *1 Thessalonians 5:16-18 AMP Rejoice always and delight in your faith; be unceasing and persistent in prayer; in every situation [no matter what the circumstances] be thankful and continually give thanks to God; for this is the will of God for you in Christ Jesus.*

Try this Gratitude Countdown

- **What are five things worth thanking God for right now?**

Before You Ever Had The Problem, God Had The Solution.

- **Who are four individuals that have shown me love in some way?**

- **What are three mistakes I am glad that I have not made?**

- **What are two of my best memories from this past year?**

- **What is one blessing I expect to be grateful for this time next year?**

Week Six – Day Five
Essentials For Living In Faithful Excellence
Gratitude Fuels Joy

The Problem

Every year around January 10th, 12th, or 13th, millions of people experience one of the most disappointing days of the year. That's right, not even 1/12th of the year has passed, and they wake up to realize they are a loser. They're not really a total loser, just not the official winner in the Annual New Year Powerball Lottery. On January 13th, 2021, approximately 600 million people discovered they did not win the 1.6-billion-dollar Powerball. To date, it is the largest ever. But for the three winners from Tennessee, California, and Florida, oh, the joy! There were a few other smiling faces among the 73 individuals who were 1-million-dollar winners and the eight individuals who won 2 million dollars. Now, I am not advocating the lottery in any way. In fact, that is the most foolish way to go after wealth. (See the stories of lottery winners who have had life crashes after winning). My favorite part of this story is this little side note. At the 7-11 Store in Ono Hills, California, where the winning ticket was sold, hundreds of people were standing around cheering and taking selfies with the store clerk who sold it, so they decided to enter and share his joy.

I had a major life revelation of a serious problem a few years ago. I had lost some of my joy. In my opinion, losing any joy is losing too much joy. It's a little three-letter word that we sing about and hear about, yet it is something most people want more of in this life, yet it eludes most people in this world. How about you? Could you use more joy? The problem we will look at today is part of a journey God has been taking me on for the past few years. I'll admit I have not arrived, but this "Joy Journey" has changed me and continues to change me. Joy is not a distant destination at which we arrive one day. Rather, it is a path we choose to take each day. I believe it is in the DNA of everyone born of God. Joy may include happiness, but it is so much more. Joy doesn't mean my life is perfect or I never have any problems or challenges. The joy I am talking about doesn't depend on circumstances. Rather, it is present, available, and powerfully at work regardless of what may be happening now or how the future may appear. Let's look at the most fantastic solution from the most joy-filled person I know.

The Solution

Jesus not only lived a joy-filled life, but he also had some powerful things to say about joy as well as some amazing words written about His joy. In **John 15:11,** He says, *"I have told you these things so that My joy and delight may be in you and that your joy may be full and complete and overflowing."* Then, in **John 16:24,** He says, *"Until now you have not asked the Father for anything in My name; but now ask and keep on asking and you will receive, so that your joy may be full and complete."* And finally, in one of my favorite joy verses, Jesus says in **John 17:13,** as He is praying for His disciples, *"But now I am coming to You; and I say these things while I am still in the world so that they may experience My joy made full and complete and perfect within them filling their hearts with My delight."* We see the following truths from these verses and so many others.

- **Jesus was identified by joy (also see Luke 10:21)**
- **Jesus modeled a life of joy for us (also see Hebrews 12:2)**
- **Jesus wants us to experience His joy and pray that we do.**

Furthermore, according to **Romans 17:13**, joy is one of the three characteristics used to describe His Kingdom (righteousness, peace, and joy). Then, according to **1 Thessalonians 5:16-18,** Paul instructs us to *"Rejoice always.... For this is God's will for you who are in Christ Jesus."* Could it be that one of the reasons Jesus wants His joy in us and our joy made full is because it is such a powerful magnet to draw people to Him? The scriptures often say of Jesus, *"He greatly rejoiced..."* which is defined as feeling or showing great joy or delight. I don't believe we can accurately represent His Kingdom or effectively advance it without His joy. Joy is a powerful force when He is our source of joy!

One of the hindrances to experiencing joy in our lives is the reality that we have an adversary, the Devil, who has plans to kill, steal, and destroy our joy. This is an area where we must reject passivity and take responsibility to stand against this enemy. Being proactive for more joy also means *"Being careful then how you live, not as unwise, but as wise,"* as **Ephesians 5:15** states. True wisdom means getting rid of any "stinkin' thinkin" and taking every thought captive to make it obedient to Christ (see **2 Corinthians 10:5**). Consider that all of us average about 50,000 thoughts daily. That is either good news or bad news, depending on the types of thoughts you think. And most of those thoughts are reruns and replays of previous thoughts. So, back to wisdom. What you let in your thoughts shapes your mind, which shapes your beliefs, feelings, values, expectations, and eventually your actions.

Before You Ever Had The Problem, God Had The Solution.

Do you see the progression and why it is so vital for our joy level that we be ruthless and vigilant about guarding our heart as we are encouraged to in the book of wisdom (**Proverbs 4:23**). Here are three not-so-wise ways that we can disrupt and destroy our joy.

1. Absorbing and soaking in the wrong stuff
Our environment, exposures, and experiences can often be our worst enemy.

2. Dwelling on our defeats, deficiencies, and disappointments
Remember, where we dwell, we swell!

3. Neglecting what matters most
When we are so focused on what we don't have, we forget what we do have. As the saying goes, you may have hundreds of problems, but you also have millions of blessings.

Let's get back to some solutions. Here are two simple habits to help restore, sustain, and increase your joy.

1. Renew your mind daily
What does God say in His word about you, your circumstances, and His power in you? (see Proverbs 4:23 and Luke 6:45).

2. Practice a grateful heart daily
This is a choice you can make and a direction you can take to live in God's will for you. (see 1 Thessalonians 5:18).

Remember yesterday's reading on gratitude? Gratitude is like a mental gearshift that takes us from complaining to contentment. It is the practice of relentless praise and thanksgiving, which is the doorway and access point to God's presence. That is where you find more joy than you will ever need, and it will always be available to you if you are a child of God. The seed thoughts we plant in our hearts and the words we release from our mouths will send us either soaring toward joy or spiraling down away from it. The fullness of joy does not come from getting the perfect job, finding the ideal mate, winning some Lottery or HGTV Dream Home, or even everything going your way. It's when God shows us the path of life, and we choose to walk in it. Because in His presence is fullness of joy! (see **Psalm 16:11**). This unrelenting joy is God's gift to you and me. So, do you want more joy?

The Truth

Take a few minutes to pray through the following verses and consider how God desires you to know His joy and for your joy to be made whole. (I've intentionally included more verses than in previous days because I really want you to have more joy!)

> *Psalm 16:11 NKJV You will show me the path of life; In Your presence is fullness of joy; At Your right hand are pleasures forevermore.*

> *Psalm 51:12 NKJV Restore to me the joy of Your salvation, And uphold me by Your generous Spirit.*

> *John 15:11 AMP I have told you these things so that My joy and delight may be in you, and that your joy may be made full and complete and overflowing.*

Before You Ever Had The Problem, God Had The Solution.

John 16:24 AMP Until now you have not asked [the Father] for anything in My name; but now ask and keep on asking and you will receive, so that your joy may be full and complete.

John 17:13 AMP And now I am coming to You; I say these things while I am still in the world, so that My joy may be made full and complete and perfect in them [that they may experience My delight fulfilled in them, that My enjoyment may be perfected in their own souls, that they may have My gladness within them, filling their hearts].

Romans 14:17 NIV For the kingdom of God is not a matter of eating and drinking, but of righteousness, peace and joy in the Holy Spirit,

1 Thessalonians 5:16-18 NKJV Rejoice always, 17) pray without ceasing, 18) in everything give thanks; for this is the will of God in Christ Jesus for you.

Hebrews 12:2 NKJV looking unto Jesus, the author and finisher of our faith, who for the joy that was set before Him endured the cross, despising the shame, and has sat down at the right hand of the throne of God.

Week Six – Day Six
Essentials For Living In Faithful Excellence
Keep Changing, Keep Growing

The Problem

The only difference between a rut and a grave is the length and depth. Plus, it's easier to get out of a rut than it is a grave, so keep that in mind as well. Have you ever seen someone in a rut or found yourself in one? You usually don't get there by accident and it's a potentially dangerous place to be. It often starts with falling into a comfortable groove where it's easy just to coast along. Former football coach Lou Holtz said, "In this world, you're either growing or dying." Growth is a lifetime process and a daily decision. We have already talked about intentional living, one of my favorite subjects, and one thing that has dramatically impacted every area of my life. Charles Schultz's beloved comic character Charlie Brown said, "I think I've discovered the secret of life – you just hang around long enough to get used to it." The problem with that approach is once you get used to it, it changes again.

Here is an essential life truth that poses a problem for many – "Change is inevitable, but growth is optional." I'll admit I have a love-hate relationship with change, and maybe you do too. I love it when it benefits me, and I hate it when it doesn't. I love it when I initiate it, but not so much when it comes from someone or somewhere else. I recently read this from a humorous book of ineffective motivational sayings.

Before You Ever Had The Problem, God Had The Solution.

"It's never too late to change. So just wait until you absolutely have to." Again, this is not a good strategy for growth or life. Amid this growth and change problem, here is some good news. Growth is optional but also possible and primarily up to you!

Simply put, growth doesn't happen by accident, and hope, as wonderful as it is, does not prove to be an effective strategy for growth. A time comes when we must choose to stop hoping to become that person we want to be and start taking steps to be that person. It's imperative that you are intentional about growing in any area of your life and be deliberate about it to the degree that your life depends on it because, well, it does! With that in mind, let's look at a solution.

The Solution

Regardless of where you are in your growth journey, I believe God is more than able to provide the solutions to get you to where you need to be and ultimately want to be. Life was not meant to be lived in a rut, yet even the best of us can find ourselves there at any point. I want to encourage you to see each day as an opportunity to grow. As I type these words on my laptop, looking out my sunroom office window, I see two palm trees, and they remind me of one of my favorite scripture passages, **Psalm 92:12-15**. I have since personalized it and turned it into a confession that I speak over my life regularly.

> *Psalm 92:12-15 AMPC "Father God, You will cause me to flourish and thrive as I choose to walk uncompromisingly righteous; to live long, upright, being useful, fruitful, majestic, stable, and incorruptible.*

I will be planted in Your presence, and I will grow in grace, still bringing forth fruit in my old age, full of spiritual vitality and rich in love, faith, peace, and joy.

By Your steadfast love and Your power at work in me, I will be a living memorial to show that You are faithful to Your promises – that You are my rock and there is no unrighteousness in You."

I believe that when I declare this and pray it over my life, I am expressing to God my heartfelt desire to stay passionate and flourish in my faith. I am choosing growth over stagnation and thriving rather than just surviving. It's a practical step of faith to shake off setbacks, disappointments, hurts, and discouragement. Instead, plant yourself in God's possibilities.

Maybe you've heard this saying, "Some people quit living at fifty, but we don't bury them until they are eighty." These people have lost their joy and so much more in life. Don't let that be your story, path, or destiny. God has purposes and promises for you that will bring you to a flourishing finish as a testimony of His faithfulness! This is the growth I am talking about and something we all can go after as we eventually graduate from this earth.

One of my favorite people at John Maxwell Company is Roddy Galbraith, who trains and mentors our coaches to become better speakers. He always closes his emails with this bit of encouragement that I love – "Stay humble and hungry." We remain humble, knowing that we all need to grow, and hungry being committed to doing it. I encourage you to accept that encouragement and keep growing. In the future, you will be glad you did and may even thank me one day.

The Truth

Do you remember this simple truth? *We are always only one decision away from a totally different life – for better or for worse!* Is there a decision you need to make today about your personal growth? Do you believe God has good plans for you? For your growth? For your future? Consider the following verses and make an intentional decision today about your growth.

> *Luke 2:52 NLT Jesus grew in wisdom and in stature and in favor with God and all the people.*

> *John 10:10 NKJV The thief does not come except to steal, and to kill, and to destroy. I have come that they may have life, and that they may have it more abundantly.*

> *Jeremiah 29:11-13 NIV For I know the plans I have for you," declares the Lord , "plans to prosper you and not to harm you, plans to give you hope and a future. Then you will call on me and come and pray to me, and I will listen to you. You will seek me and find me when you seek me with all your heart.*

> *Psalm 92:12-15 NLT But the godly will flourish like palm trees and grow strong like the cedars of Lebanon. For they are transplanted to the Lord's own house. They flourish in the courts of our God. Even in old age they will still produce fruit; they will remain vital and green. They will declare, "The Lord is just! He is my rock! There is no evil in him!"*

2 Peter 3:18 AMPC But grow in the grace undeserved favor, spiritual strength, knowledge and understanding of our Lord and Savior Jesus Christ the Messiah. To Him be glory, honor, majesty, and splendor both now and to the day of eternity. Amen and so be it!

Before You Ever Had The Problem,
God Had The Solution.

NOTES

Week Six – Day Seven
Essentials for Living in Faithful Excellence
Reflect, Record, Rejoice

Reflect

Review the past 6 days of devotionals and reflect on what stood out to you from what you read. Did you get any new insight? Any new understanding of God's word? Did you discover any areas of your life where you need some solutions?

Record

Write down your thoughts from what you just reflected on, putting down any impressions you received on paper or in digital format. Ask God to give you insight into what He wants to show you from what He has spoken to you this past week.

Rejoice

Take time to express thanksgiving and praise to God for His Word, for His desire to speak to you, lead you, and give you solutions for living in faithful excellence. Make an intentional effort to find someone today with whom you can

Before You Ever Had The Problem, God Had The Solution.

share what you learned from your time with God this week in these readings, your prayer time, and most of all, through His Truth!

Afterword

Asking questions is a great way to get answers and solutions. Asking the right questions is even better. I wrote about this subject back in Week Two, Day One. Asking good questions is essential to determine where you are, where you want to be, and who you are and want to be. Jesus was a master at asking the best questions. He asked the most critical questions, such as:

- **What does it profit a man if he gains the whole world and yet, loses his soul? (see Matthew 16:26)**
- **Can any of you, by worrying, add a single day to your life? (see Matthew 6:27)**
- **Do you believe I can do this? (see Matthew 9:28)**

So, the question for us would be, "Do you believe God has the solutions to life's problems?" "Do you truly believe Jesus can give you the solution to whatever problem you are presently facing?" The premise behind this little devotional book has been simply this - "Before you ever had the problem, God had the solution."

When we go to the One who is all and knows all, we can discover those solutions. That one is Jesus Christ. He invites us to come to Him daily in prayer, seeking His face, receiving His wisdom, being filled with His spirit and power, loving Him, and enjoying Him forever. The disciples who spent the most time with Jesus when He walked this earth as a man asked Him one of the most important questions in the Bible. Luke 11:1 says, "*...One of His disciples said to Him, Lord,* *teach us to pray."* So, in one of Jesus's most significant messages for solutions in life, He teaches the disciples (and all of us) to pray. In this passage (see **Matthew 6:9-13** and **Luke 11:1-4**), there are seven solutions to seven problems most of us face in life. Consider the following:

1. God's solution to an inferiority problem is His person

The most important thing about you is how you view God. As Matthew 6:9 says, *"Our Father in Heaven…"* is the best place to start. A.W. Tozer famously said, "What comes into our minds when we think about God is the most important thing about us." When we begin with the correct view of Him, we get a proper view of us. That starts by viewing God as your faithful, loving, and powerful Father who cares deeply for you as his child.

2. God's solution to confusion is His plan

"Who am I? Why am I here? Where am I going? Why is this happening to me?" Those types of questions can be overwhelming and confusing. The solution Jesus gives us to pray is *"Your kingdom come, Your will be done on earth as it is in heaven."* (Matthew 6:10). That is submitting to His plan and purposes for your life, and you can be confident they are good.

3. God's solution to worry is His provision

When Jesus said in verse 11 to pray, *"Give us this day our daily bread,"* He was telling you the solution to worry, anxiety, and stress over your needs in this life is trusting in Him to provide for your health, your finances, your present, your future, your everything. He is more than able and always trustworthy. Daily prayer for daily provision is a daily solution that we have available each day.

4. God's solution to guilt is His forgiveness

The first step in being free from guilt is admitting that we have all sinned and none is perfect. We have all made mistakes, maybe have some regrets, and even hurt others. This needs healing, and Jesus gives us a solution in this prayer. He says to pray, *"Forgive us our sins as we forgive those who sin against us."* (See Matthew 6:12). This powerful solution is only experienced when we choose to receive His forgiveness and grant forgiveness to others. This decision leads us to solution number five.

5. God's solution to strained relationships is His peace

Life's biggest problems are often "people problems." Relationships go awry when we hurt others or they hurt us, intentionally or unintentionally. Frequently, words that are said in anger or bitterness take root, and as Hebrews 12:14-15 describes, it eventually "defiles many." The solution from Jesus in Matthew 6:12 is to *"forgive those who sin against us."* Again, start by receiving forgiveness from God, and then you will have the grace and power to forgive others. We all need His power at work in and through us to let go of the past, have His peace in the present, and move forward into the future He has for us!

6. God's solution to temptation is His protection

When you pray, *"Lead us not into temptation but deliver us from evil..."* as Jesus taught in Matthew 6:13, we ask for His protection, which He loves giving His children. If you are a parent, you understand this, as there probably isn't anything you wouldn't do to protect your child. God knows how vulnerable we are to temptation, and He desires to ruthlessly protect and defend you when you call on him as your Father.

7. God's solution to fear is His power

In Matthew 6:13, Jesus closes his teaching on prayer with this confession, *"For Yours is the Kingdom and the Power and the Glory forever. Amen!"* There is no reason to fear when we are a part of His Kingdom of righteousness, peace, and joy (see Romans 14:17), filled with the Power of His Holy Spirit (see John 7:38-39) and His glory made known through us. (see Matthew 5:16 and 1 Corinthians 10:31)

Jesus confirmed that in this life, we will have problems, frustrations, troubles, distresses, etc. (see **John 16:33** AMPC). I love that He gave us a realistic picture of life and also said in that same verse, *"...But take heart (be courageous, confident, undaunted and filled with joy) for I have overcome the world and have conquered it for you."* Jesus has always been, is right now, and always will be *The Solution* we all need. So be encouraged, my friend. Before you ever had the problem, God had the solution!

Appendix
Tools And Resources

Scriptural Affirmations and Confessions
(See Week 5, Day 5)

Two Confessions By Pastor Peter Lord
Taught To Park Avenue Baptist Church

Confession #1: "I Am"

> *"I am an awesome spirit being of magnificent worth*
> *as a person.*
> *I am deeply loved by God, I am fully pleasing to*
> *God,*
> *I am totally accepted by God, and I am absolutely*
> *complete in Christ.*
> *And when my person is expressed through my*
> *performance, the reflection is dynamically unique.*
> *There has never been another like me in the history*
> *of mankind. Nor will there EVER be.*
> *I am an original! One of a kind! Really somebody!*
> *And so are you!"*

Confession #2: "My God And Father"

> *"My God and Father, You are my faithful Father.*
> *You will keep all the promises you have made.*
> *You will keep the general promises of Scripture and*
> *the specific promises given by the Holy Spirit to me.*
> *I will not focus on appearances.*

Before You Ever Had The Problem, God Had The Solution.

I will not limit You to my time schedule.
I will not expect You to do it my way, for Your
ways are not my ways.
I focus on You, my heavenly Father.
I concentrate on your faithfulness.
I confess that all your promises are "Yes" because I
am in Christ Jesus.
I acknowledge Your ability and desire to perform
what You have promised.
I rejoice and give You glory for the fulfillment of
Your promises to me.
You are my Father and God.
You are my faithful Father.
You are my powerful Father.
You are my loving Father.
Thank You!"

Confession #3: "A New Day Confession"

Today is a new day
Therefore;
I refuse to be shackled by yesterday's failures.
What I don't know will no longer be an
intimidation. It will be an opportunity.
I will not allow people or circumstances to
determine my
Mood (attitude)
Method (how I conduct myself)
Mindset (my self-image and God-view)
Mission (purpose and calling)
I will pursue a mission greater than myself by
adding value and blessing to at least one person that
I encounter each day.

*I will have no time for self-pity, gossip, or
negativity from myself or others.*

Personalized Scripture Prayer Blessings

Based on Numbers 6:24-27; Isaiah 60:1; John 17:13 and Philippians 4:6-7

*The Lord bless you, and watch guard over you and keep you
___(insert name here)_____. The Lord make His face shine
down on you, His smile rest on you, and His Glory rise upon you to
enlighten you according to **Isaiah 60:1**. May He be gracious, kind,
and merciful, giving you His very own abundant, undeniable,
unrelenting and unprecedented favor.*

*The Lord lift His approving countenance upon you; His delight in
you, His pleasure over you, and His joy in you, on you and through
you made full according to the very prayer of Jesus for you in **John
17:13**, and may He give you His peace according to **Philippians
4:6-7**, to garrison and mount guard over your heart and your mind
in Christ Jesus. And He will put His name on you and bless you!
(declare the provisions of His Name).*

Based on 1 John 3:1-2; Jeremiah 29:11-13; Ephesians 3:16-21 and Galatians 5:22-23

*Now, may God, your faithful Father, your loving Father, and your
powerful Father, look you full in the face today.*

*May He cause you to prosper, flourish, and thrive in your physical
body – every joint, ligament, muscle, bone, nerve ending, tissue, and
organ aligned with God's healing and strength.*

Before You Ever Had The Problem, God Had The Solution.

May your soul (mind, will, and emotions) be washed and cleansed by His Word and Truth.

May your spirit be ignited by His fire and His power at work in you both to will and do His good pleasure, producing His spiritual fruit of love, joy, peace, patience, kindness, goodness, gentleness, faithfulness, and self-control in you and through you to others.

Based on Psalm 92:12-15

Father God, You will cause me to flourish and thrive as I choose to walk uncompromisingly righteous; to live long, upright, being useful, fruitful, majestic, stable, and incorruptible.

I will be planted in Your presence, and I will grow in grace, still bringing forth fruit in my old age, full of spiritual vitality and rich in love, faith, peace, and Joy.

By Your steadfast love and Your power at work in me, I will be a living memorial to show that You are faithful to Your promises – that You are my rock and there is no unrighteousness in You.

The Benefit and Blessing of a Personal Life Mission Statement

Do you have a personal life mission and purpose statement written out or recorded and available for reference, representing your core values and who you desire to be? If you don't, I encourage you to take the time to discover and develop that document. Many free resources are available to create this extremely valuable tool, which can serve as a life navigation guide, keeping you moving toward the person you feel called to be.

Here is a link to an excellent one from my friend Dan Miller, creator of "48 Days To the Work You Love." https://www.48dayseagles.com/get-worksheets

I have included my life mission statement on the following page. I crafted this living document over 30 years ago, and although I have slightly edited it over the years, I pray through it almost daily. I have found this to be one of the most important gifts for my Life Leadership on every level. Mark Twain initially said, "The two most important days in your life are the day you were born and the day you discovered why."

This is my "why," do you know yours?

Personal Life Mission Statement for Billy Durham

My mission in life is to **Seek** *God with purity, passion, and perseverance; to* **Gaze** *on His glory, majesty, and power; and to* **Dwell** *in His presence, under His protection and according to His purposes 24/7. I am fueled by courageous* **Faith***, compelled by outrageous* **Love,** *and empowered by contagious* **Hope.**

I am a passionate and engaged husband committed to loving my wife as Christ loves the Church, His bride, by cherishing, honoring, and seeing her as holy. I am a faithful and focused father committed to loving my kids and grandkids as Father God loves me by enjoying them, imparting to them, nurturing them, and encouraging them into their mission and destiny.

I am a leader with a vision guided by values, influence established by integrity, and perseverance motivated by purpose. Because of Jesus Christ and His power at work in me, I will be a faithful son and a fruitful son as well as a faithful soldier and a fruitful soldier in His Kingdom. I am anointed and appointed by the Holy Spirit to invite, equip, and lead others into a life of **Communion** *or Abiding in Christ* **(Ps. 27:4-8; Mt. 22:37-38)** *and* **Conquest** *or Advancing His Kingdom* **(Mt. 22:39; LK 4:18-19).** *Through Jesus Christ, I have been given everything I need in body, soul, and spirit: talents, gifts, abilities, resources, and relationships to fulfill my mission. (Therefore, I refuse to make excuses for not fulfilling this call)*

More Books By Billy Durham

1. The Cup and The Sword: Pursuing a Life of Communion & Conquest

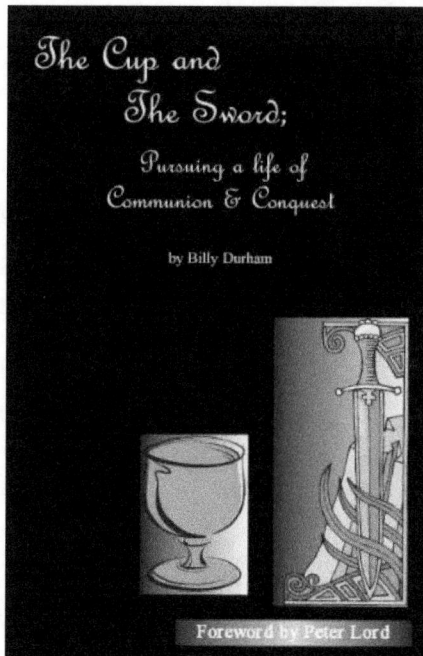

Before You Ever Had The Problem,
God Had The Solution.

About The Author

Billy Durham has spent over 43 years on a life adventure serving in student ministries, missions, music and worship, executive leadership development, and personal growth coaching through multiple venues and associations. He has provided leadership in conferences, churches, mission projects, seminars, and retreats in North America, Central America, the Caribbean, Asia, and Europe. Most recently, Billy served in several roles on the Staff Leadership Team for Park Ave Baptist Church in Titusville, FL., for more than three decades. He has now embarked on a new adventure of helping others find L.I.F.E. Leadership Solutions through his continued association with The John Maxwell Team as a certified founding member providing personal coaching, speaking, and training.

Most importantly, he shares this adventure with his amazing wife of 38 years, Sherri, as they now reside on the west coast of Florida, and as she continues to graciously laugh at his jokes, together loving God and enjoying Him forever. They have three adult Children, who, along with their spouses, have provided (to date) four amazing grandchildren. This would be the source of some of the real joys in their lives.

Billy received his undergrad degree from the University of Georgia in Music Therapy/Music Education. He also studied at Western Conservative Seminary, located in Portland, OR. His ministry highlights include serving in part-time or full-time ministry staff positions at eight different churches, one para-church ministry, Christian Bands, guest speaking, music performance, worship leading, leadership development and training at conferences, retreats, and special events for over four decades. He is a certified coach, speaker, and trainer with the John Maxwell Team, joining as a founding member and receiving multiple certifications, including Parent and Family Leadership. He is the designer and developer of the Elijah-Elisha Leadership Institute, which mentors and trains young adults in leadership and personal growth. He has collaborated on other writing projects, including the Embraced Heart Youth Journal (a Youth Edition prayer journal based on Peter Lord's "2959 Plan") and "Knight's of the Cross," a student discipleship tool produced by Morningstar Ministries.

As someone with a life-long passion for personal growth and who encourages and equips others for their individual spiritual growth, Billy continues to speak, lead, mentor, and train others in this process. Along with his wife Sherri, a Christian Counselor certified in Temperament Therapy, they provide marriage mentoring and coaching for couples to connect greater and thrive in their marriages through individual sessions, retreats, and events. Billy has another book, "The Cup and The Sword, Living a Life of Communion and Conquest." This book takes the reader through the discovery of some practical ways to abide in Christ (Communion) and advance His kingdom (Conquest) by doing the one thing that matters most.